I0558788

WHAT IS SCHOOL FOR?

A Manifesto
for Parents

JESSICA ZOU

For every child

Title: What Is School For? A Manifesto for Parents / Jessica Zou

Published in the United States by States of Matter, Inc.

Copyright © 2024 by Zou, Jessica, Author.

All rights reserved.

No portion of this book may be reproduced in any form without written permission from the publisher or author, except as permitted by U.S. copyright law.

Book Cover by Henry Yiu.

Book layout and illustrations by The Reluctant Illustrator.

1st edition 2024.

Contents

It's wonderful to meet you!

I'm glad you're here.

A poem from the Carbon Almanac Network reminds me of you, reader.

You Have Power [1]

You have more power than you think.

You matter.

Because you can organize. You can communicate.

You can establish standards for how we live and for what comes next.

Your ancestors are proud of you. The seven generations to come are grateful.

You may feel like a small drop in the ocean, but together we create currents

of change. Systemic change happens with multiplied action.

You.

You matter.

Just ask a kid.

---

1. "You Have Power," The Carbon Almanac, accessed November 5, 2024, https://thecarbonalmanac.org/you-have-power

Introduction

It took two years of volunteering in the leadership team at my son's school to learn that no decision in the public school system was straightforward or simple.

I had been worried about our neighborhood school for some time, fearing that I had made a mistake somewhere.

My worries lessened when I heard David Guggenheim's advice in his documentary, *Waiting for "Superman."*

"The best way to support our public schools is to attend one in your own neighborhood."

Yes, I wanted to support our public schools. And yes, I wanted to support our neighborhood and community.

But now, here I was: mourning the loss of our art program, feeling both frustrated and disappointed alongside the other parents. I couldn't help but wonder what we could do to make it all better.

Our school was divided, and unlike other parents, I had an added challenge to face. I had just joined the Building Leadership Team (BLT), and if I chose to stand with the parents by arguing with the administration, I would become the sole front-and-center target within the leadership team. If I chose to follow the school's authority, I should simply walk away from my parent representative position on the team, right there, right then.

I chose to stay in the BLT. But throughout the effort of getting the art program back, we encountered a subtle but persistent attitude from all parties in the system: the art program seemed important, parents' voices were declared to be important, but neither of those was important enough for the system to make a change.

The path forward seemed gloomy. I was overwhelmed with fear and uncertainty. I was so discouraged by the challenge that I started to question if it was the work I should be doing after all.

And I wasn't alone.

If you are a parent like me, you've had a lot of questions about your children's school, why things happen the way they do, and what drives those experiences. You are among hundreds, even thousands of families experiencing school in their own ways, and that same system is how you received your education as a child. Schools haven't changed much since you were there, yet for some reason, things aren't working out the way they should. Your children aren't thriving as you imagine they could. Despite reassurance from the well-meaning folks at the school and within the Parent-Teacher Association (the PTA), you know something isn't right.

In all you try to do, and everywhere you look for answers, you are seeking peace of mind that your children are in good hands. You want to make sure they are on the right path to success, past their school years into a future that's full of possibilities. And yet, you find yourself or loved ones constantly in disagreements, lodging complaints, and even escalating into conflicts about what's not working at school. Instead of peace, you and your children are experiencing emotional distress, fear, frustration, and hurt, which further affects their school environment.

Not only is change desperately needed, but the list of what needs to be changed has become overwhelmingly long: mediocre outcomes, a decreasing sense of safety (both emotionally and physically), and a polarized community, to name several. The past few decades have seen a steady enrollment decline, accelerated by COVID-19, which further complicated funding struggles for public schools and eventually led to school closures across the country.

So when I ask "What Is School For?", I want to be clear that it is a multifaceted topic encompassing several broad aspects including personal growth and development, academic needs, and economic and societal factors. The complexity of the school system and the challenges surrounding it often leave people feeling stressed and overwhelmed. Often, it leads to the belief that the system is too big, and little can be done to change it, no matter what's not working. And a partner belief is this: we are too small or insignificant to influence change to that degree. These beliefs are understandable, but nothing could be further from the truth.

Change is possible. First, we need a framework to help us see and understand our schools and how they work.

It wasn't until I started to write this book that I realized I was creating a process to understand the school system as if I were branding it. This is how I help businesses and organizations reveal the purpose for their existence, help them see their core services, identify their survival challenges and opportunities for success, and create messaging that is consistent between what they say and what they do.

I am offering you this framework as a lens to see the school system more clearly.

How can you decide what's best for your children, your family, or your community? When can you trust your experiences, and when does it create blinders around your ability to see clearly? How can you make small but effective changes without needing the system to change first?

What is school for?

Whenever we are faced with layers of challenges, doubts, opportunities, and choices, we need to know where to look, which questions to ask, and what to evaluate.

In this case, we need to understand what's really going on within the school system. For example, a good captain is experienced with icebergs, how sea ice behaves, and the best practices for navigating icy waters. Rather than focusing on the tip of the iceberg—the symptoms—they work to understand the entire system of icy conditions in deep water. If we learn what school is for, how the education system works, and best practices for navigating human learning beneath the surface, we get to see what's driving our children's school experience, whether or not it's working.

The purpose of this book is to do just that: to explain how the school system works, what our children need to succeed in school, and what might improve their educational experiences and outcomes.

I am proposing a general approach and potential solutions for improvement. You can use it to support your children, advocate for change in your schools and local community, and better understand how to 'be the change' for this movement.

But this book is NOT about political debates. I am sure there are plenty of people out there who are more qualified to do that.

This book is also NOT about finding an individual or organization to blame, but seeking the collective solutions that will help our children and their schools.

Losing the art program was a catalyst event I experienced with the school system. As we will learn together, it was just a symptom that can guide us to go deeper. You might not care about art programs (although I hope you will change your mind about that by the end of the book), but that's not the point. Once you see how interrelated each factor is, and how we, as parents, contribute to our children's school journey both in positive and negative ways, you can replace the art program with your own experience, trace those symptoms down to their root cause, and draw your own conclusions about what to do next.

Layer by layer, we will see the system as a whole.

In my interviews with parents, I realized most of them had no problem coming up with their own answers to the question "What Is School For?" But very few had learned to see how their school would answer.

Until we learn to see our schools for what they truly are, we can't say we agree with what they are here for.

Chapter 1:
The Catalyst

I still don't know how the news got out.

The 2019–2020 school year had just ended—the fourth year at our neighborhood school for my son and our family—leaving parents and children with an extended break to process what the pandemic had done and still might do. Schools had moved everything planned for the physical classroom to the online world, which barely worked, especially for smaller children. We needed to sit with them to manage their technical difficulties and monitor their naturally short attention spans. The amount of screen time, parent involvement, and online homework had been taxing for everyone.

The next school year, my younger son began kindergarten in an online environment. By the end of the year, his unfinished online homework numbered over 100 items, and none of us had the energy to get them done.

It was amid these circumstances, with parents trying to put the tears and frustration of the school year behind us, that we learned we had lost our art program.

It was like a bomb got dropped on our usually quiet neighborhood.

As a parent representative for the school's Building Leadership Team (BLT), I was immediately pulled into the heated discussions among parents. People were beyond angry.

"Who made the decision? How come we didn't hear anything about it?"

"After all the volunteering and donations, is this what we got in return?"

"My children are so upset about losing art. It was their favorite subject!"

"Is it too late to get it back?"

I had no answers for them; I hadn't even started my role in the BLT yet.

A few months earlier, a friend approached me offering all the volunteer positions in the PTA (Parent-Teacher Association): the president, the vice president, and the parent representative for the BLT. I turned it down at first because I had struggled in school. Not when I was a student, but as a parent. On the surface, I had volunteered in the classroom and at school events as much as I could for the past four years, but I wasn't sure how I felt about the PTA. I couldn't figure out how to show up—how to be both grounded in who I was and fit in or be helpful to other parents at the same time. I had questions about our school, the PTA, and how everything worked. Lacking clarity made it challenging to step forward any more than I had to.

Then the pandemic started, and our city went into lockdown. The whole world stopped. Physical schools were no longer available, and everything was moved online.

Like everyone else, I did a lot of inner work amid the pause. For the first time in my life, the outside world became a true danger. Everything "out there" was filled with a deadly virus, and the question of life and death was closer to us all "in here" than ever. Inevitably, I came to this question: if tomorrow were to be my last day on earth, what would I regret?

It was such a sad question. I thought about my children and their lives in the world without me. I thought about the challenges they would face. The virus, the unpredictable climate, the polarized society we have become, the misinformation and mistrust, all the complicated issues that divide us, and for sure, many more than I could imagine today.

I also realized that, for this moment, I would regret not paying enough attention to my children's schools. If I had a chance to do something to help prepare our children for the future but didn't take it—if I kept looking away instead of staring at the problems head-on—I would regret it.

Meanwhile, my friends who had served in the PTA were helping the organization find candidates for upcoming vacancies.

In the business world, when the top leadership positions in an organization are empty, it is safe to assume something much bigger is going on. It would have been smart to walk away, and the obvious choice if I had been looking for something low-stress and easy to do. But I was neither smart nor seeking something easy. I ended up taking the position and prepared to take on my role with intention.

Finding My Place

Like many moms, I cared about my children's education from the moment they were born. But as a first-generation Chinese immigrant, I grew up in a very different public school system and society. Education is highly valued in Chinese culture; in many ways, great education was thought to guarantee success in life. For many families, the definition of success is measured by the children's good grades, acceptance into good schools, prestigious universities, and eventually, highly respected careers such as medical doctors, lawyers, professors, government officials...

When my son was little, I heard about how smart and talented other people's children were, and I was beyond amazed. They could read and write at a young age and figure things out before they were expected to. As toddlers, they played with all kinds of puzzles, could put letters in alphabetical order, and started to read before age three.

When I took my child to Gymboree at twelve months old, I was dying to learn how amazing he was. As the months rolled on, we found classes for music, art, dance, gymnastics, swimming, reading, math, you name it. By four, I signed him up for piano lessons—the only thing he showed any real interest in—and my days were filled with driving from class to class. Looking back, this was partially because I wanted to learn what he was interested in, and partially because I had no idea what to do with his early education.

Meanwhile, despite all the amazing stories I heard from other parents, my son didn't talk until he was three. As hard as I had worked to give him every opportunity possible, I was still afraid that he missed valuable learning opportunities because of something I neglected. I was afraid of regrets.

In the last year of preschool, the teacher handed us his assessment tests on math and reading. My husband and I were devastated by the results. We were so troubled, we signed him up for a tutoring service, hoping he could improve in both subjects. By the time he started kindergarten, he caught up on math but was still below grade level on reading. That same year, I learned about volunteering opportunities in school and what the other parents did to help the children. I wanted to be part of that world—until I realized it wasn't as easy to navigate as it seemed.

Looking back, I tried many things with my son partially because I wanted to learn about him and his interests to help him connect with things he enjoyed. But it was also partially because I had little knowledge about this unfamiliar school system.

By the time he turned eight, I decided to step back from so much "doing," to understand my experiences. And I started to see the school environment in a different light.

It sounded like schools had their arms wide open for us to participate in our children's education. But when we finally mustered the courage to get through the front door, the sense of community and belonging that we had hoped for was nowhere to be found. Speaking up or being honest with ourselves often felt like a treat rather than an expectation.

For example, the parent representative role in the BLT is the least accessible to parents (though it also turned out to be the one no one wanted). Few parents know about the existence of the

Building Leadership Team, let alone a parent role on the team. And while it's a place where parents should be able to equally participate in important school decisions with the teachers, staff, and principal, it was also challenging to be in that position. Because when the rubber hits the road, things can be rough for everyone on the team, especially for parents.

Volunteering is a form of civic engagement that supports our public school system, but this volunteer role was unknown to outsiders in our school until we lost the art program. I couldn't understand exactly *why* it was hard for parents like me to be ourselves, or why it was challenging to participate and speak up, especially if our schools really did want our support.

I couldn't see the "right" path forward, but I had an opportunity to advocate for my son, and I wanted to take it. The only question was—how?

It wasn't until I came across Jacqueline Novogratz's book, *Manifesto for a Moral Revolution*, and her course with Acumen Academy that I learned the concept of "just start." She said this:

> *"There is only one way to begin. Even when you are not clear what your purpose is, how you can make the most impact with your life, or the path ahead feels overwhelmingly elusive, just start—and let the work teach you."*

It turned out to be the best advice I've heard.

With this in mind, I went back to my friends in the PTA and asked if there was any position left to be filled, and there was. The one that was the hardest to access. The one that nobody wanted. The parent representative for the BLT.

Building Leadership

The BLT is usually made up of the principal (the captain), teacher representatives (at least one for every two grades), a classified staff representative, a specialist representative, an instructional assistant representative, and a parent representative. Except for the principal, every team member serves up to two years in the BLT. All the public school employees are paid to work in the BLT, and the parent representatives are volunteers. Despite lacking compensation, parent representatives have equal voting rights in all decision-making processes.

According to the bylaws in our school, the main goal of the BLT is to make collective recommendations that would guide and influence academic achievement and outcomes for other employees to vote on. Considered one of the governing bodies at our local school, the BLT takes on responsibilities around decision-making, advocacy, financial supervision, and strategic planning to support the school and families.

Little did I know, the first thing I would face as the BLT parent representative would be attempting to save something that we had already lost.

As soon as I agreed to be the parent representative, my friends told me there were challenges to work through in the role, especially around decision-making. The BLT parent rep is one of the most impactful volunteer roles because of the decisions we make as a team including budget, program, staff allocation... you name it. But there is rarely enough time for parent representatives to connect with the other parents, get their feedback, and represent them.

Votes usually happen in two or three days, which makes sense for teachers and staff since they work in teams and mostly stay connected on a daily basis. But it's nearly impossible to hear a diverse range of parent voices, collect potential feedback, or evaluate BLT proposals sufficiently in that amount of time. I didn't understand why we were in such a hurry, especially for budget decisions. Wasn't it important to take some time to listen to families and evaluate all our options? Didn't we want to make sensible decisions with everyone's voice in mind?

Adding the loss of the art program to those ongoing stresses gave me an emotional introduction to the BLT. Not only was the outcome at odds with families, but nobody had cared enough to understand what the impact might be on their children. Families weren't given a chance to ask the BLT to reconsider. The lack of transparency created distrust between families and schools, undermining the picture of a school "community" that both the BLT and PTA were trying to paint.

Searching for Answers

It shouldn't be a surprise that losing a program over the summer—and a difficult summer at that—had a great impact on the community. Some children felt they lost one of the few things they actually enjoyed and looked forward to at school. Some parents felt that our children's education had gotten worse overnight. It wasn't just art we had lost, of course. Some other teachers were gone, and other changes here and there had been made—but losing art had the stronger and more direct impact on our children, who were already facing a tough year. It felt impossible to fight for everything, so we decided to focus on saving the art program.

Before we decided what to do next, we wanted to find out if the program was savable. The whole community was buzzing with conversation. Communications with school authorities were brewing. The sense that our kids were entering a school year filled with uncertainty, loss, exclusion, and who knows what else, rushed through our minds. Yet, there was so little we could do to make it better. So few people in the school seemed to care about our kids—or us.

With the faintest bit of hope that all of us coming together might be enough to create change, we decided not to give up. A few well-connected parents organized a group that could work toward a solution. These parents knew the system better than most parents, and they reached out to every single person they could think of. They included the superintendent's office, legislators, the district school board...and me. Nobody knew what would come of our meetings or if it was even possible to reverse our situation.

As the newest member of the BLT, I reached out to our school principal because I wanted to hear his thoughts. He was open and honest about everything, including the systemic regulations and rules that affected the budget, as well as the personnel dynamics associated with the decision. Soon, parties outside our school agreed to meet and listen. Slowly, parents became hopeful again.

The director of the school district's board sympathized with us but suggested we reach out to others for a solution. There was nothing she could do to reverse the situation.

The legislators were next in line. Based on their previous experiences, proposing any bills related to the budget had been extremely difficult to navigate with the state and had never been successful at all. They suggested parents ask some other organizations if they had money to give to supplement the budget.

The superintendent's office told us that, since the decision was made by our local BLT, they would respect the building's decision and would not intervene between the school and parents. Our request was back to the school for resolution.

We had now gone full circle and were back at ground zero. It looked like none of the parties in positions of power actually *had* the power to make a difference. I couldn't help but wonder: in this gigantic public school system, what needed to happen for parents to save the art program for our children?

Not getting any results didn't make parents go away. Instead, we had more questions that needed answers. Why couldn't our school split the full-time position between art and music like others had? Why did we have to choose one over the other?

A Split Decision

Eventually, we learned that the BLT held a strong opinion that students were better off with a good music program that had a full-time teacher than if the budget were split between part-time music and art teachers. The decision to let the art program go had been a unanimous one for the previous BLT team as well as the leaders of the PTA.

The angriest parents had the opposite argument: of course, art was the better option. Credible research even showed that art was more accessible for children than music—and it's especially true for children from low-socioeconomic households. There were just as many children in the community who would prefer the art program over music.

As I mentioned earlier, my kid connected with music more than art, but my professional experience with marketing agencies and designers (my husband for one) has taught me that art is needed and equally important.

Our school was divided.

Amidst the arguments between opposing sides, a third voice showed up. A few parents wanted to promote a volunteer-based art program to fix the problem, believing that having something for students to do would be better than nothing at all.

By the end of the community meeting, our school agreed to allow a parent-volunteer-led art program as a compromise, by allowing parents (usually one to two people with or without teaching experience or backgrounds) to go into the classroom and teach art with an informal curriculum. At the micro level, it seemed like a reasonable solution—many parents felt grateful at first, since a filled gap was better than nothing. Even though they felt something wasn't quite right, they couldn't put their finger on it.

Parents who weren't convinced by the compromise saw the issue at a macro level. When looking at the bigger picture, they saw this third option as the most harmful and dangerous to us all. Not only did it undermine children's and parents' requests for an art program, but well-intended volunteer work left learning needs unmet. This contributed to the core challenge our school was up against: we were racing to the bottom, away from quality learning experiences and the outcomes those would demonstrate.

Given how conflicted we were even among ourselves, I couldn't help but wonder: what did the word "advocacy" mean in today's school system anyway?

Chapter 2:
Welcome!

Even before I started my parenting journey in public school, I had many questions. If parents cared about our children and their learning, did that mean we had to care about everything else in the school as well? I had no idea what to expect from teachers or classes. Was I alone in that? Who could answer—I mean, really answer—parents' questions?

I was in my mid-thirties when Sebastian was born. This was considered late to have children in Chinese culture. My husband and I hadn't really talked about it, because my sales job had me traveling several times a year for business. We just didn't have time to consider it. But my mid-thirties felt like the last train for children, and it was time to decide whether to jump on or simply release the thought.

When I did become pregnant, we both agreed I would stay at home. When my husband's family first came to the US, his sister watched him most of the time since both their parents worked in restaurants. He mourned as he explained, "They were barely there for us. I don't want the same thing for our kids." I was grateful that he could take on the financial challenge of meeting the increasing needs of our growing family and glad to provide time and attention to our kids in return.

There are many differences between cultures in the US and China. But the biggest one is individualism vs. community-based societies. Because of my expectations around the community, I carried assumptions about schools into Sebastian's early years. I expected to find the warmth and genuine welcome of the community that schools claimed to be.

Our first experience in school was at a little preschool near our neighborhood where my son attended for two years.

Like many preschools in the country, it was privately owned and operated, a well-loved space that felt intimate, safe, and approachable. Parents followed the school's lead for participation and support during events. The friendly environment made it possible for families to feel good about interacting with the school and each other. This experience furthered my expectations for the community and gave me some confidence about navigating future schools.

"I can do this," I said to myself. "If the public school system is just like this, we're going to be okay."

Culture Shock

When it came time for kindergarten, the public school with the higher rating and reviews fell outside of our geo zone. We were told that we could put our son's name on the waitlist in case any seat became available, but he was not automatically eligible to attend. So, we signed up on the waitlists for that school and two others, since our neighborhood school wasn't known for its performance on standardized test scores, hence the lower rating.

Soon after, we learned that Sebastian didn't gain a seat in the schools we preferred, but that most of his preschool friends had. Now our son was going to be separated from his friends, including his best friend, and starting all over again from scratch, in a school that we wouldn't have chosen for him. We were disappointed, but there was nothing we could do about it. I had heard that US schools were excellent at nurturing children's confidence and offering more freedom, so I hoped that the scores wouldn't be all that mattered.

As summer drew to an end, we looked forward to our first-ever meet-and-greet event in the neighborhood school he had been assigned to. It was the first time our family got to see Sebastian's kindergarten classroom and meet his teacher. We were excited to embark on this new milestone in our lives.

As soon as we walked into the building, we were greeted by a group of volunteers who politely guided the traffic by the front door. Behind them, a greeting wall with the word "Welcome" was surrounded by translations in many different languages to reflect the demographics in our community. More than 60 percent of the students were kids of color, and from the moment we saw that greeting, I believed that our school actually wanted us to feel welcomed. I believed their celebration of diversity was not a wish, but a reality.

Meeting the teacher was the most exciting part. Teachers were already proving they cared about our child the same as we did. That not only made us appreciate the work they did but also want to support them as best we could. Thinking back to the community-based society I grew up in, I also knew that nothing fulfilled me more than real human connection through genuine conversations. Having some one-on-one time with the newest teacher in Sebastian's life was an important moment for us.

His teacher was polite and excited to meet him. And after a short greeting, she turned to another family and asked about their child.

I noticed how relaxed the other parents were. It seemed like their conversations flowed like a river. *Look at how they enjoy themselves*—I wished I could be just like them. Instead, I began thinking about the first impression I made. Did she like my child? Did I do anything to change that? I couldn't help but feel a little worried.

After the classroom visit, we joined other families on the playground for a potluck hosted by the PTA. It was intended to give us the chance to socialize and connect while we ate, but that's not what happened. Just like all the other parents who arrived at the playground before us, my husband and I found a quiet place to sit while the kids played. My body tensed up as each set of parents ate alone, without speaking to anyone.

Meanwhile, the ladies who had guided us through the entrance earlier gathered in the middle of the playground, in front of everyone, talking and laughing as if nobody were watching.

Among them, I noticed a parent I had met through Sebastian's preschool, whose children were older than ours. I got excited, thinking I finally saw someone we actually knew, and I wanted to say hi. But she was part of that group of volunteers. What if she didn't remember me—a newcomer who knew nothing and nobody here? I suddenly felt timid and nervous. The seemingly short distance between the edge of the playground and the group of volunteers felt like a canyon too big to cross. It was easier for me to give up the thought of reconnecting than to walk up to her and risk embarrassing us all on the first day.

The warm feeling I had gotten from the preschool was nowhere to be found. I didn't want to hold onto a negative first impression any more than I wanted to create one, so I brushed it off as if I didn't notice it at all. I couldn't help but wonder—why did I want to feel warmth and a sense of belonging here? Maybe it was normal to not feel included in public school? I didn't know. But for the next six years, this feeling somehow persisted.

Learning about American culture had always been part of my studies in universities, working as a sales professional, and eventually a brand marketer, and living in this country for decades. But it was different when I became a mom and stepped into the public school system.

The public school culture was different from anything I had experienced before. It was both puzzling and unpredictable, especially to someone like me who knew so little about it at that time. Understanding the cultural differences and assumptions I observed may help you, my dear readers, see where I came from and where I am going—hopefully, alongside you.

Cultural Differences

Over time, little by little, I found my way in the US public school system. This journey has been filled with highs and lows, happiness and sadness, joy and tears, and plenty of good friends. At first, however, I was just confused. Comparing the US school system and the Chinese school system I grew up in would be like comparing apples with pears. However, knowing there are clear differences helped me look at school itself from a different angle and ask questions I might not have otherwise.

I have thought long and hard about these differences and ultimately realized that there is no straightforward conclusion about which is better and which is worse. Each is simply a different way of seeing things. To demonstrate, I have distilled these differences down into three categories: intensity or rigor, system structure, and volunteering.

Intensity/Rigor

The Chinese schools I grew up in operated with absolute authority. It was the school's responsibility to teach children. Their slogan—meant for everyone in the community to follow— was "study hard and make progress every day." The curriculum and teaching methods were designed not only to fulfill government requirements but also to create accountability for the school's requirement to produce results.

Chinese schools also reflected historical values. Works from Confucius and Mencius to political leaders were included in the curriculum, as well as moral, community, and societal values. When I researched moral values in education, I found other Asian countries and surrounding areas—such as Taiwan, Singapore, India, South Korea, Pakistan, etc.—have similar curricula.

Both US and Chinese schools highly value memorization and repetition, and they both believe testing is an important measurement of student success. But for Chinese schools, it's a common belief that longer school hours, more classes, tons of homework, and rigorous testing often lead to higher scores. Chinese students' average study time commitment is fifty-five hours per week, far beyond an international average of forty-four.[2] In 2018, the Programme for International Student Assessment (PISA) performed a global assessment of over ten million fifteen-year-old students from seventy-nine countries, and Chinese students outperformed their peers in mathematics, reading, and science.

Even with the outcomes it has created, this kind of intensity has led to major consequences for children's physical and mental health, especially the latter, and received sharp criticism and backlash from students, parents, and Chinese society in recent years. The 2018 PISA survey showed that even though Chinese students topped the chart for performance, they landed in the world's bottom ten countries on life satisfaction.

This points to another consistency that I have seen across the board: what works for some children does not work for others. Maybe the real question is not how rigorous our schools should be, but how can we redefine rigor so that every child has what they need?

System Structure

In Chinese schools, both the administration and the teachers belong to the same organization—the local school. School principals are elected from a combination of the teachers' nominations and the system's approval. Principals are also given the authority and responsibility to hire their school team, including all the teachers and staff members, and there is no tenure for teachers within those teams or any other positions.

Parents in our neighborhood school in the US were shocked when they learned that, in our school, the principal belongs to the school administration, while the teachers belong to the teachers

---

2. This is a quote from the Wikipedia article about the Double Reduction Policy, a policy attempting to address the stress associated with this level of student engagement. https://en.wikipedia.org/wiki/Double_Reduction_Policy

union. In other words, the principal and teachers are employed through different organizations.

There are benefits to this kind of structure, but challenges as well. Having two organizations might balance power dynamics in processes such as decision-making when governing our school, but the flipside comes when the two parties don't agree. When the teachers and the principal are at odds—and they often are, sometimes in unresolvable conflicts—it puts students and families in the middle of the controversy and affects the school as a whole.

Volunteering

Parents are not active participants in the Chinese school system. In fact, schools were built with walls and gates to separate the campus from the outside world. Parents were only occasionally invited to schools for parent-teacher conferences and some special events. Schools had strict rules about visitation, and the homeroom teacher was the recommended contact point for parents to communicate with schools.

Instead of parents, students were volunteers in schools: taking turns to help with tasks in their classes such as collecting homework, helping teachers, organizing events and activities for the class, drawing posters on the bulletin board, cleaning classrooms and public areas, etc. This expectation that everyone should work together created a sense of community and togetherness among the students. This, combined with an ongoing community-based society, made it natural for parents to expect warmth and genuine welcome from schools and each other whenever they did come together for school events.

Unlike the PTA, parent volunteering in China is limited to trivial things such as contributing to the classroom needs, but not participating in the school leadership team, let alone the voting right to make school-wide decisions. The country didn't have a parent involvement history like the PTA in the US. Advocacy isn't the norm in schools. Without parental involvement making some kids more visible than others, students have the opportunity to feel that they are equal—in the same way that schools require uniforms to minimize comparison.

This realization brought me to a new question: When we volunteer in our US schools, do we know where volunteering stops, and advocacy begins? Do we think of them as separate matters at all?

Organizing events like meet-and-greets, fall festivals, or movie nights were considered volunteering. But fighting for the art program was different. It was more than volunteering. Meanwhile, there were many interactions with the PTA, like our very first meet-and-greet event, where I couldn't help but wonder—if the PTA is meant to advocate for all the children in the school, wouldn't that group want to meet the parents? Wouldn't they want to include everyone they would represent?

When we lost the art program for the 2020-2021 school year, the PTA agreed to let it go without attempting to get feedback from the greater parent group. When the parents decided to fight the decision, the PTA remained silent. This didn't stop parents from advocating for the art program, but I couldn't help but wonder if this was how the oldest and largest child advocacy association in America, the PTA, had been operating.

I began to question if there might be a difference between *advocacy* and *volunteering*. If there is, what is it?

I turned to the internet, and Wikipedia gave me these descriptions, with the emphasis mine:

*"Advocacy is an activity by an individual or group that **aims to influence decisions** within political, economic, and social institutions. Advocacy includes activities and publications to influence public policy, laws, and budgets by using facts, their relationships, the media, and messaging to educate government officials and the public."*

"Volunteering is a voluntary act of an individual or group **freely giving time and labor, often for community service**. *Many volunteers are specifically trained in the areas they work, such as medicine, education, or emergency rescue. Others serve on an as-needed basis, such as in response to a natural disaster."*

Advocacy is about educating and influencing government officials and the public, whereas volunteering focuses on task fulfillment—getting the work done. In other words, 99 percent of the time at our neighborhood school, the PTA parents are volunteering for the school rather than advocating for our children.

Finding Common Ground

In six years at our neighborhood school, both the school and the PTA have repeatedly used the word "community" or the phrase "building meaningful relationships" in their communications with parents. Yet losing sight of others or being unwilling to empathize with other people's needs is the main complaint parents have had about the PTA.

Walking back to the parking lot with my husband and children after the kindergarten meet-and-greet, I felt small. That feeling has stayed with me since and in a profound way. It nudged me to ask questions about everything that we did or were asked to do. It shaped the way I served on the BLT, because when one person among us feels small, it hurts us all.

This turned out to be another cultural assumption that I carried with me. Growing up in a community-based society, building social harmony was both a goal and value, even in sports. A popular Chinese mantra is "friendship first, competition second," to remind children that competition isn't for the purpose of winning but to build partnerships beyond the games.

As the phrase "community-based society" suggests, community forms the building blocks of the greater society. An intricate relationship between individual and family, community and society, not only defines how we view ourselves and others around us but also how we see and understand the impact that one person has on the rest of the community.

This is the sense of camaraderie, partnership, and belonging that I was looking for when we met the other parents at Sebastian's school, but I wasn't sure how I could find it. Besides the fact that our children attended the same school, there were barely any feelings of community among us.

I thought the discomfort I felt at school stemmed from my being a newcomer and an immigrant, unfamiliar with our school and the public school culture. But after six years of being in the system, this feeling never changed even though I wasn't a newcomer anymore—even though other people came and went. There seemed to be an underlying belief about who should be accepted and who shouldn't, about whose voice mattered and whose didn't. No matter what level of parent leadership I participated in, I couldn't seem to change that dynamic. But deep inside I know, the truth about community is that it is interdependent—what affects one affects us all.

During my term as the BLT parent representative, I attended the state-level PTA legislative assembly. It was two full-day events, held virtually because of COVID, to vote on the top issues to send to the state legislature. Another parent and I joined the assembly together, not knowing what to expect. Even though we registered for the event on time, it wasn't clear to me how or by whom the issues were proposed or evaluated to get on the final agenda. We were simply given an agenda and the ability to vote yes or no.

The top issues that year were related to the pandemic but were both about funding: "increasing access to nursing, mental health, and social-emotional learning staff; and supporting students and preserving education funding." Funding is a big topic and can be a book on its own. In 2024, when the district made school-closure proposals to the public, funding was listed as one of the reasons for the decision. Funding is important. In this book, we will look at deeper causes that lead to issues we face today, including funding and a perspective for change.

Something about the assembly didn't feel quite right, and I didn't know what it was at the time. When I started to write this book, I realized what I was missing: our kids. The purpose of everything we do—the purpose of our schools—was not taken into consideration.

Budget and staffing matter, but why didn't anybody talk about how our schools were meeting our children's learning needs? No one tried to find out parents' true concerns about our children and our schools. No one tried to hold our schools accountable for their learning outcomes. No one was advocating for learning.

***

When I first saw the amount of volunteer work there was for parents to get involved at our neighborhood school, I mistook the work itself as advocacy. Contributing to the classroom, supporting teachers, and helping out at events weren't an issue for me—both as a stay-at-home mom and professional. But I struggled to see the purpose behind it. The more I did, the more I fell in line with the volunteers and the PTA, and the more I fit in. But my child was still struggling with school, and other children and their parents still weren't seen or heard.

Events matter. Volunteering matters. But if that was the only thing that PTA and parents could do, who was advocating for our children's learning needs? If we couldn't influence something so significant as losing an art program, was the BLT parent representative any different from volunteering?

Before we move on, let's make this clear about advocacy: speaking up for children is complex. Children are the ones who actually receive the school services that we advocate for, but many children often don't know what they need, or they can't fully speak up for themselves about what they need. Age and growth increase that capacity; what is even more important is to have an environment that nurtures and encourages children to be themselves. When speaking up for oneself is at odds with the environment that emphasizes and rewards compliance, fitting in, and discipline, it becomes more challenging to nearly impossible. We often see that by the time children have the knowledge, understanding, discernment, and courage, not only have they grown out of the system, but they are parents of their own children, beginning the cycle all over again.

Rather than trying to compare what works or doesn't work between the US and Chinese school systems, there's something we share as parents. Something more powerful than anything a system can provide. Something we forget when we get caught up in school politics and conflicts. When we're feeling small in front of the system, we have forgotten to trust the one thing we know: the relationship we have with our children.

When Sebastian's teacher handed us more assessment tests that showed him lagging, my husband and I felt the pressure to create even more educational opportunities for him by engaging in a tutoring service. But Sebastian was starting to fight back—and fight hard—about all the classes that I put him through. Tears, frustration, and resentment. That was the moment I realized my idea of education didn't work for him. I took a big step back, feeling defeated—like I'd failed. Again. I questioned myself, my judgment, and my capability of getting things right.

Parenting is hard. But being a parent to my kids taught me a lot about them: what makes them happy, what makes them sad, what makes them excited, and what makes them afraid. We are not always right, but my husband and I are the closest people to them who can even begin to understand. Parents sometimes believe they don't know their children well enough to speak for them, but I bet you know enough to tell when something isn't working. You know when your children aren't happy. Only you have the emotional connection and heart-centered memories of them at their brightest to know when they genuinely find joy in something, and when their light is being dimmed. And that knowledge is gold.

Joy is a universal indicator that something is working for us as humans, and children are no exception. When school works, children experience joy—maybe not happiness about every little detail of their workday, but genuine joy about being themselves in an environment that genuinely welcomes and cares for them.

On the playground at the meet-and-greet, I thought the PTA parents knew the secret—like they had everything figured out or were naturally immune to all the struggles many of us had, and simply enjoyed the community and successful experience that I craved. But when I look back on my journey over the past six years, I learned that even the seemingly powerful and influential parents in the PTA felt small and excluded in our school just like I did. So maybe what we all want is a lot more similar than we thought: a real connection wherever we go. Not the illusion of influence or power we can gain, but the depth of understanding that what we all really care about is our children and their learning in school.

Studying vs Learning

Chapter 3:
Studying vs. Learning

Have you noticed how school scenes in film or TV are always about kids who are not interested—often with someone in the classroom napping on the desk, even drooling? I don't know about you, but those scenes remind me of hot afternoons at my desk, fruitlessly fighting with my heavy eyelids, yet scared to death that I could be called out in front of everyone any second.

Whenever I couldn't submit homework as a child, the teacher and my parents were the most upset. I wasn't nearly as bothered as they were because there was a reason that I couldn't turn it in:

I didn't understand the content.

I needed more time and help.

I was afraid to make mistakes and be wrong.

Those things bothered me. But not the deadline.

Once, my mom asked me, "Who do you think your homework is for?"

I said, "You."

She turned red.

So, I changed my answer: "Ms. Chen." Still not what she expected.

She couldn't believe it.

Once, I was upset about my kid not turning in their homework. The same scene repeated itself, only this time, I got to ask the question: "Who do you think your homework is for?"

Remi, my second grader, blinked his eyes and said, "Ms. M."

I raised my eyebrow. "What?"

"You!"

I couldn't help but burst into bitter laughter.

He was right.

A Learner's Perspective

When we are required to do something that we are not interested in or don't understand, it's hard to feel good about doing it. When we don't feel like we are doing the homework for ourselves, we simply do it to avoid being punished.

Besides blaming my sleepy younger self or scolding my children for not paying attention, I had never thought about why struggling so much in the classroom seemed to be the norm. Studying was something that we simply had to do. Homework is something another person wants from us. This is what school is supposed to look like.

But then, Sebastian's teacher assigned a project to the fifth-grade class: pick a subject that you are interested in, make a poster telling us what you've learned about it, and decorate it the way you would like.

He went full out. For a kid who usually complains about writing assignments, he wrote on every space he could find, right up to all the corners and edges. The poster was filled with words and drawings about Megalodon, a kind of shark that I know nothing about. I don't know how his work was received in the classroom, but he didn't seem to care about that at all. He was so proud of himself and his work that not only did he show it to us but took the time to explain it and wait for our questions.

For parents who have outgoing children who enjoy sharing, you might not think this is such a big deal. But to us, it is huge! He didn't share anything else about his days at school. If we pushed hard enough, he *might* mumble "I dunno." This project was entirely different than anything else he had done at school before.

We tend to believe that sending our children to school means they are receiving an education, which necessarily includes studying and learning. As long as our children go to their class-rooms, follow the teachers' instructions, and do their homework, that's all there is to school.

But this project showed me something new. Something I needed to pay attention to. Something surprising: **studying** and **learning** are *not* the same thing.

The two words mean very different things, and this realization changed how I looked at everything else from then on.

A Learner's Perspective

When we have choice and freedom, we are drawn to things that are naturally interesting to us. We know what we are curious about and want to know more. When our curiosity leads the way, we find out what we didn't know before and learn something new about ourselves and the world around us.

The Center of Studying

While real-life learning involves much trial and error and learning from our failures, failing to study, or failing at studying, means failing a test. And there is no positive spin to that. It is a one-way street.

Nobody studies to fail.

The word "study" has its origins in Middle English and Old French. The Middle English term was *studie*, which came from the Old French word *estudie* or *estude*. These, in turn, were derived from the Latin word *studium*, meaning eagerness, zeal, or diligence.

In Latin, *studium* was closely associated with the concept of devotion, enthusiasm, or pursuit of knowledge. The verb form *studere* meant to be eager or zealous for, especially in the context of learning or education. This later evolved to mean acquiring knowledge through reading, investigation, or contemplation, and it's now primarily associated with education and research.

As I began to differentiate studying from learning in the school environment, I saw studying as having the following criteria:

a. Studying isn't about choice but rather compliance with grade-level standards.

b. Studying is graded and tracked on report cards.

c. Studying meets specific school and system goals instead of the students' personal goals.

In a study-focused environment, students often ask questions like, *"Will this be on the test?"* That's the value of the lectures, homework, and all the effort worthy of investment in our current school model: a chance at passing a test and moving on to the next one.

Understandably, students would only care about what's on a test. Fully absorbing a concept enough to get it can be difficult or impossible for many students. If we don't get a chance to ask questions along the way, by the end of the lesson we can feel so lost that we don't even know what to ask anymore. And it's nearly impossible to have the time right there, right then to understand something new—along with digesting what the teacher has said and connecting it to our own knowledge and experience. By the end of class, we often feel lost like we're standing in no man's land. If we can't figure out the homework, our confidence may be so low that we spend what's left of our energy hiding and playing small.

To add to the frustration, when what we study isn't connected to our actual life, we often wonder: why bother?

Memorizing information and practicing through repetition serves the final goal of taking the test, and nothing else. Once the test is done, we are done studying, and that's how most of us finish our school years.[3]

A Learner's Perspective

When there is too much information jammed into each class, it's hard to remember and follow, let alone process and digest. Instead of dumping everything all at once and expecting us to just get it, give us breaks—time for us to process, ask questions, practice, and have the incremental assessing points to make sure we have a solid base to build new information upon to help us comprehend and internalize.

Measuring Success

Unfortunately, tests are the only way for the public school system to measure the results of students' studies, and studying is the only way for students to pass tests.

Early on in my time on the BLT, I learned that every elementary school in the public school system has a master plan—a North Star—to follow. Not many parents know about this, even though it is a public document available for everyone to see. In

---

3 Samuel Suresh calls this "regurgitation" in his YouTube video called "Own Your Learning," which is worth looking up and watching. https://youtu.be/br0jghA4JEw?si=ry9V6QQVjYDNBKIo

our school district, it's called the "Continuous School Improvement Plan (CSIP)." Every school in the system has one.

To find it for yours, type your school name and then "continuous improvement plan" into a search engine. If you can't find it online, reach out to your school and ask for it. It's meant to be shared with all students and parents.

Once you find it, look for "Priorities and Measurable Goals" (or a similar title). The following are real examples from our local schools:

- *3rd Grade English Language Arts (ELA) Priority Goal: For the 2020-21 school year, at least 41 percent of 3rd-grade students of color furthest from educational justice will meet standards or higher on the ELA Smarter Balanced Assessment.*

Note: the same pass rate, 41 percent, applies to the 2021–2022 and 2022–2023 school years.

- *Safe and Welcoming Environment Priority Goal: For the 2020–21 school year, the students will demonstrate a Year-To-Date Attendance Rate of at least 95 percent.* [4]

Two things are worth noting here: 1) The listed pass rate is a close reflection of the pass rate of all students even though it is emphasized here as "students of color." 2) Our school system uses attendance rates to measure whether we have a "safe and welcoming environment." We will talk more about this in the coming chapters, but it's important to remember that there is a reason this is the only measure of safety and a welcoming environment.

- *7th Grade Mathematics Priority Goal: For the 2020-21 school year, at least 41 percent of 7th-grade Students Furthest from Educational Justice will meet standards or higher on the Math Smarter Balanced Assessment.*

---

4   As of May 2024, this measurement has been updated to "by June of 2024, 83 percent of Black students will respond favorably to the statement 'At school, I learn how to speak up for what I need' or a similar question around self-advocacy, up from 75 percent in 2022."

- *9th-grade students of color furthest from educational justice will accumulate sufficient credits (6+ or more) to be on track to graduate in 4 years.*

When I asked former public school teachers about these numbers, some waved their hands and dismissed the goal by saying, "Yeah, but I never follow that."

Whatever a teacher is doing within their classroom, I can assure you this goal is the only compass that guides decisions on budget, staff, support, and everything else. Test results measure studying effort, and the way to achieve those goals is to mark attendance. As long as kids show up, take notes, ask about what will be on the test, turn in their homework, and—at least half of them, anyway—pass, the school is satisfied.

A Learner's Perspective

When we get low grades, we are stressed about them. We think we're not smart, or we can't learn, or that other kids are smarter than us. Teachers favor students who have good grades and don't make trouble. If we don't get good grades and aren't popular, it's hard to feel liked or welcomed by our teachers or peers. And then it's hard to want to show up.

Avoiding Failure

One of the phrases that my older son loved to say throughout his elementary school years (and still sometimes today) is, "I win." He hated losing. Sometimes he got upset and burst into tears, and other times he would try to do everything he could to prevent the loss and avoid the pain.

As much as I understand the excitement of winning and the pain of losing, I had a hard time comprehending the deep impact losing had on him. Doing things that we are certain about and comfortable with feels good, but that's not what life is all about. In *Hidden Potential*, Adam Grant says this: "Playing only to your strengths deprives you of the opportunity to improve on your weaknesses."

If we only choose to do the things that we are certain we can win, then what will we miss in the things we aren't sure about?

Similarly, if we believe that every human being is unique and intelligent in their own way and learns at their own pace, then what does testing really measure? And what are we missing in the children who don't thrive in that particular testing model?

A Learner's Perspective

There are many ways to draw a picture, write a story, make a pie, compose a piece of music, or strategize on the football field. We don't know which color, process, ingredient, or play works for us until we try them out. Learning is not a guarantee that something will work but a choice that we make—a commitment to show up and go through the process, and a revelation about something unknown to us before.

The Heart of Learning

The word "learn" has its roots in Old English. It is derived from the Old English word *leornian*, which means "to get knowledge, to be cultivated." The Old English term itself has Germanic origins, and it can be traced back to the Proto-Germanic root *liznojan*—related to the idea of obtaining knowledge or skill through study, practice, or experience.

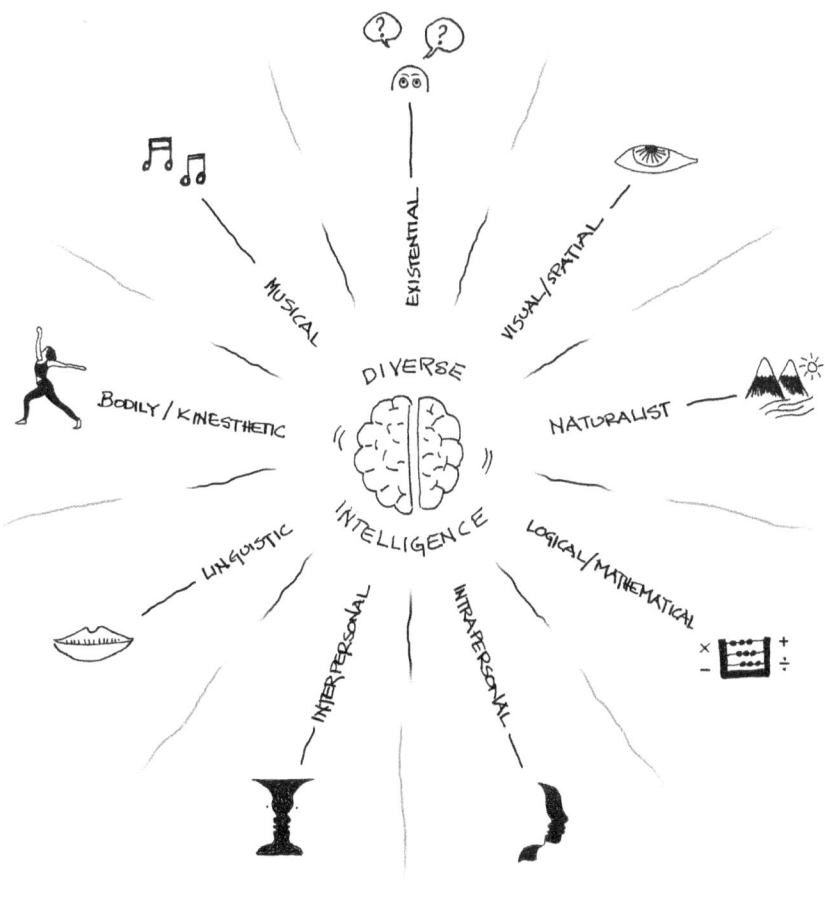

Diverse Human Intelligence

This figure illustrates the various types of learning that Sir Ken elaborated on in his talk. It is based on Marc Vital's 9 Types Of Intelligence - Illustrated: https://www.behance.net/gallery/18024715/9-Types-Of-Intelligence-Illustrated

Existential: tackling the questions of why we live and why we die
Visual/Spatial: receiving, understanding, and manipulating visual information and space
Naturalist: understanding living things and reading nature
Logical/mathematical: quantifying things, making hypotheses and proving them
Intrapersonal: understanding yourself, what you feel, and what you want
Interpersonal: sensing people's feelings and motives
Linguistic: finding the right words to express what you mean
Bodily/Kinesthetic: coordinating your mind with your body
Musical: discerning sounds, their pitch, tone, rhythm, and timbre

This root is also connected to similar words in other Germanic languages, such as the Old High German *lernan*.[5] Eventually, "learn" came to represent the acquisition of knowledge, skills, or information through various means, including study, instruction, and personal experience.[6]

Based on this definition, learning is broader than studying. Yet we often hear people interchange "studying" and "learning," and in the school system, they are used casually. The overlap in use between learning and studying is not only confusing but also fails to distinguish the important differences between the two. Because of these unclear distinctions, many of us mistake studying for learning.

An important way to see their difference is from the learner's perspective, like the ones I have included throughout this chapter. It's a crucial lens to have, especially in a school environment. In schools, studying often shows up as memorization, repetition, and regurgitation for tests. It is how students comply with standards and assessments, and it has little to do with themselves. And while studying is about compliance, learning is a process of self-connection. It is curiosity-led, interest and passion-based exploration. A learning project solves the challenges in ownership, motivation, and enrollment—or wholehearted buy-in—that commonly make studying a challenge for most students.

With this perspective, we begin to see the importance of stories like the one Sir Ken Robinson shared about Gillian Lynne.

In 2006, Sir Ken Robinson gave a TED talk about schools that drew nearly 75 million views.[7] In it, he told the story of Gillian Lynne, the choreographer of two of the longest-running shows in Broadway history, *Cats* and *The Phantom of the Opera*.

---

5. You can follow this etymology progression here:
   https://en.wiktionary.org/wiki/learn

6. Credit to Merriam-Webster's online dictionary.

7 Watch Sir Ken Robinson's TED talk, "Do schools kill creativity?" here:
   https://www.ted.com/talks/sir_ken_robinson_do_schools_kill_creativity

He explains that he interviewed Gillian about the start of her dancing career, but instead, he discovered a remarkable story. In the 1930s, the school wrote to Gillian's parents saying that they believed she had a learning disorder because she couldn't concentrate, she disturbed the other children, and her homework was always late. She was eight at the time—third grade.

Gillian's mother had no choice but to take her to see a specialist. Twenty minutes after the conversation with the doctor, he told Gillian that they were going to continue their talk outside of the office and asked her to wait in the room by herself. If Gillian had been seen by a different doctor that day, they might have diagnosed her, put her on medication, and told her to calm down. Instead, before leaving the room, the doctor turned on the radio on his desk.

The minute the door was closed, Gillian was on her feet, dancing to the music.

The doctor asked Gillian's mom to watch her daughter for a few minutes and told her, "Mrs. Lynne, Gillian isn't sick. She is a dancer. Take her to a dance school." And she did.

Gillian said, "I can't tell you how wonderful it was. We walked into this room, and it was full of people like me—people who couldn't sit still, people who had to move to think." She learned all kinds of dances, eventually auditioned for the Royal Ballet School, and then enjoyed a wonderful career at the Royal Ballet. She not only became a multimillionaire from her efforts, but she was responsible for some of the most successful musical theater productions in history, entertaining millions of people.

This is not just a story about dancers, but swimmers, runners, mountain climbers, basketball and football players, and all children who "need to move to think."

From this point of view, for many children in our schools, "extras" like an art program aren't just nice to have but can be a rare learning opportunity within a long day of not being able to "move to think."

A Learner's Perspective

Learning requires choices. I'm not interested in doing this, but I am interested in doing that. If I don't get to try things, I don't know what I am good at.

Learning is doing something, creating, setting a goal, accomplishing something, or at least trying to.

Learning is a way to see ourselves—who we are, what we are interested in, what we are passionate about, and where we want to go.

Unique Learning Styles

The difference between studying and learning isn't the school, the platform, the name of the program, or any fancy terms used, but whether the individual has ownership of the process or choices along the way. All Gillian needed to learn was the ability to get up and dance—to choose how and when to move as she needed to, in order to think. Of course, not everyone is a dancer, and that's exactly the point.

Contrary to the belief that paying attention to things other than studying distracts children from getting good grades, accepting children's unique intelligence brings out their confidence and a stronger sense of agency and identity. With that, they can approach their studying in a new and more successful way.

When we are interested in our learning, we want to take charge. It's fun, it's rewarding, and we are proud of ourselves for what we make and what we can do. When we feel good about ourselves for doing things that we are passionate about, we want to share our ideas with others, as well as the things we created.

Problem-Solving Skills

Seth Godin said this in one of his daily blogs: "Metaphor is the heart of learning."

It reminds me of the Chinese idiom "举一反三" from the Analects. It is translated as "learning by analogy (metaphor)" or drawing inferences from one instance to another to scale one's learning.

We can use Ikea as an example. Adam Morgan shared the story in his book, *Eating the Big Fish.* The owner of Ikea, Ingvar Kamprad, visited the Guggenheim Museum in New York City back in the day and noticed something about this unique experience. The museum didn't give visitors the choice of where they could go, but instead made everyone go up to the top, then downward past everything that the museum had on display (still without choice), then out through the shop, by the cashier, and onto the street.

He then applied that same idea in Ikea stores and their innovative room inspirations. This single change made it possible for customers to see everything in the store (which made them stay longer), which generated more purchases in the market where people tend to only seek out previously considered items.

Just like Circus Peanuts don't have nuts, Ikea has nothing in common with the Guggenheim Museum.

Some people might call it "critical thinking and problem-solving skills." Seth Godin, the Analects, Kamprad, and I say that being able to comprehend how one thing works, then apply it to something else, and make it work, is the heart of learning.

A Learner's Perspective

Listening and even understanding the lecture from the teacher only gives us their way of interpreting the concept. To fully grasp the core idea and learn it our way, we need to apply it to a project and actually do something with it. Doing helps us understand.

The Results of Learning

When I interviewed parents on my podcast, Duct Tape Rocket Ship, they frequently said they worried the most about their children's potential—their future opportunities and careers—and that's what's on their minds when they worry about their education. Our study-oriented schools measure progress and potential in test results. But is that the most effective way to know whether they will access opportunities in the future?

My friend, Mickey Horvath, hosts a podcast called The Career Guy, where he interviews people about their career changes throughout life. For the forty people he interviewed, the commonality for their success was not how well they did in school, but how well connected they were with themselves—how well they knew what they liked and what they didn't. Whenever things are not working for them anymore, they explore ways to change their jobs or forge new paths. Interests and curiosity, not rote intelligence, help people counter the fear of uncertainty that would otherwise keep them from making a change.

These are people who have learned how to learn.

Learning Develops Self-Connection

Pushing my older son to try so many new things and study with tutors didn't work out as I planned. By second grade, I had stopped everything but his usual math and reading studies in school, and he still struggled. He would try to avoid doing homework or would do it so fast that he would make many mistakes. Fighting with him to arrive at the correct answers was exhausting. Plus, I was already tired from struggling to find my path with work and life.

By the end of the school year, his grades left us no room to catch our breath. I seriously started to doubt myself. Did I really know how to help him? Was my way of parenting the best way? We both desperately needed a break from each other.

That was when I decided to take a step back from his education. No more fighting him. No more pressure. And not surprisingly, he chose to do nothing. My anxiety started to grow. I had such a strong desire to say *something* to him: *Do some math! Read a book. Any book!* I managed to hold off on that desire, but I felt even more helpless.

That year, I went back to work, and we had a sitter come to our house to stay with the children. One morning before the sitter came, Sebastian asked me how he could make a pie from scratch.

What?! I rarely baked and had certainly never made a pie from scratch. I dismissed his question and left for work without thinking much of it. But he wouldn't take no for an answer. That day, he convinced the sitter to find the information online, and together they made a dough and stored it in the fridge. The next morning, he rolled out the dough and placed it on the baking dish by himself while waiting for the sitter to show up.

Summer had come fast that year, and those days were lovely in our neighborhood. One of the neighbors had wild blackberry bushes growing in their yard and was willing to share them with the neighborhood and even strangers passing by. So, my son and the sitter harvested the blackberries from our lovely neighbor and made the filling, then baked the pie.

Sebastian has always had a sensitive palate, even since he was a baby. He could tell the difference between organic and conventional produce and voted his opinion by choosing the tastier. Growing up, he developed an interest in foods and would ask questions like, where did they come from? How did they grow? He showed overwhelming enthusiasm about our little vegetable garden by checking on their growth first thing in the morning and reporting his observations and discoveries throughout the season.

I thought it was just a little curiosity about food until he made this pie—his very first from scratch—at just seven years old. For the first time since his birth, I realized that he was making sense of the world through his relationship to food.

As we enjoyed the delicious fruits of his curiosity that evening at the dining table, I was in awe at what this simple experiment had unlocked in my son. The power of passion, the power of wanting, and more importantly, the power of joy had helped him demonstrate skills that years of school had failed to do.

We all learn through our unique view of the world. His lens is different from mine, and that is okay. It is good. He is figuring out his way of learning—like connecting the dots through food—and all I can do is accompany him along his journey. After all, he knows his perspective better than I do.

Chapter 4:
The School Environment

I have often heard parents, especially in the PTA, talk about our "school community." As much as I truly like the idea of a school that operates as a community, many of us struggle to see it play out that way.

When I met Charles Vogl, the author of *The Art of Community*, in August 2021, I asked him about our public schools. He had defined the word community as "a group of individuals who share a mutual concern for one another's welfare."

I wondered whether he saw our schools in this light, or whether it was possible to. His answer was this: If a so-called community is formed around transactions alone, and what someone can give or get from the group, it's not the kind of community that he talks about. The power of community is that everyone can be seen, heard, and understood. It's where we don't feel alone when we stay true to ourselves.

Setting aside the question of the whole school for a moment—is community possible in the classroom?

A Closer Look at the Classroom

The typical classrooms in our neighborhood school hold of rows of desks and chairs where students are required to sit down, facing the direction of the teacher, who holds the authority to determine how a subject is studied and what activities surround it. Typically, teachers do most of the talking, while students simply listen and occasionally answer questions. When COVID suddenly required virtual schooling in 2020, many parents got a chance to see and understand what was happening in their kids' classrooms. It wasn't the best example of a typical day, of course, but it was eye-opening, nonetheless.

My younger son's kindergarten classroom became a virtual call time, where they were required to stick to the screen and listen to the lecture for an hour, sometimes an hour and a half. After that, *tons* of homework was assigned on an app to make up for the short school days. When the youngest of these children returned to the physical school a year later, instead of helping them adjust to the new environment they had never experienced before, they were given a brand-new teacher on an overwhelming, unfamiliar campus in addition to what was expected from the first graders.

Sebastian, a fourth grader at that time, sat through two hour-long virtual lectures, with the students' cameras turned off unless it was their turn to answer a question. Then they had other work to complete, such as self-study and homework.

While the cameras were off and the kids were meant to be listening, my son was busy chatting with his friends. I believe the teacher had done what she could, facing an unprecedented disruption like COVID. But my son had no interest in attending the class in the first place, much less in this format. It was an exaggeration of the problems that the typical classroom setting has had all along: how are kids meant to sit through lectures and remain interested, without getting distracted, when they are barely interested to begin with?

The first time I noticed how challenging it can be to sit through a lecture, I was preparing to get back into the work-force again after my seven-year career break as a stay-at-home mom. I was accepted into a popular program at our local university, for nine months and several thousand dollars. Most of the people in our cohort were from the local big tech industry, so classes were usually at night after people got off work. Instructors were also from big tech, the senior employees who had been in the industry for decades.

The classes were taught similarly to the way kids are taught in public schools. The instructor took over the stage, lecturing most of the time, leaving a fraction of that time for group discussions amongst the students who were seated in rows facing the stage.

After hearing the same person talk for thirty minutes straight, everything started to sound the same. But that was only the beginning. The lectures usually took around two and a half hours. It was one of the most painful experiences I've had in a long time, bringing back all the memories of my difficult school years growing up—the Chinese school system was mainly studying-focused as well.

They wanted to cover a lot of content. Maybe too much. It felt like the topics were spread wide and thin. Then I started to feel bad about feeling bad—the instructors had done so much already. But even as I tried my best to listen, the minutes kept wearing on, threatening to drown me in boredom and distraction.

To fight off the helplessness, I decided to change up my participation. I began asking questions, but soon it was clear that I had more questions than the instructors expected. They made a new rule: no questions allowed until the end of the lecture.

Now that I was engaged enough to have questions, my attention turned to everything I didn't understand. Without being able to ask questions, I got so lost that I didn't even know what to ask anymore. Too much information had been jammed in for us to sort out, and now we couldn't ask for help doing so. It was nearly impossible to digest what he said and connect it to my understanding on the spot. The PowerPoint decks we were able to download only skimmed the surface of what he had to offer.

By the end of each class, I felt like I was standing in no man's land, unsure of my next steps.

I would often wonder: *Am I the only one who feels this way? Can we be taught any other way?*

But then, when the instructor would finally stop for questions, the classroom would get so quiet that we could hear each other breathing. Nobody raised their hands.

No man's land is no joke.

Ironically, without any questions, the instructor would close the class with a satisfying smile on his face, mistakenly believing the silence was evidence of a job well done.

When a classroom setting revolves around a teacher's needs, it is a teacher-centric studying model. Whether the student receives the lesson becomes secondary to the way the teacher prefers to deliver it. By the time I graduated, I was both grateful for the experience and extremely suspicious about the reputation of this fancy university—and the traditional classroom model itself.

A Learner's Perspective

Nobody seems to care about how we are doing. What might interest us? How can we stay engaged? When we are not seen, understood, or cared for, it's hard to believe we matter.

Top-Down Impacts on Environment

Four years into volunteering for classroom and school events, I still hadn't seen the school as a community. When I joined the Building Leadership Team, I was curious to know whether the inner layers of leadership would be where I'd find that connection. After all, it was a team made up of the principal, teachers, specialists, staff, and administration. Would they work together to make sure everyone felt seen and heard?

Our challenge was to find consensus among all the representatives—not just for what we wanted, but for the people we represented. Of all the meetings that this required and the responsibilities we carried, budget meetings were the hardest.

In the second year, our team was tasked with another potential cut between the music and the art programs, and because we still couldn't agree, we spent more time than what was originally scheduled to deliberate on our recommendations. The main reason that the decision took inordinately long was that neither of the programs aligned with our school goal, our North Star, or even close to what the school system focuses on.

All along, I had thought that music and the art were, or at least could be, learning opportunities for children. But since they are not the priority goal or focus, they follow a different set of administrative rules. It wasn't until I experienced Akimbo Workshops and Summit Public Schools that I learned what real learning looked like and how it worked.

The bigger problem was the same one I had found in the rest of the school system: the BLT runs on the system's rules and regulations instead of the concept of community. With administrative processes, contracts, and legal frameworks at the center of our work instead of the idea of representing a community, meetings would get intense. When the various power dynamics were at odds, they led to a hostile environment, where many of us felt unsafe and nervous about extending warmth or even the benefit of the doubt to each other.

If we couldn't come together in a small group with a shared goal, there had to be something missing at a higher level. Maybe we weren't on the same page after all.

Revisiting School Goals

Recall that there is a North Star document that the Building Leadership Team follows in order to align their decisions to the school's objectives. The "continuous improvement plan" is meant to be the foundation of consensus. But let's take another look at an example from our local school:

*3rd Grade English Language Arts Priority Goal: For the
2020–21 school year, at least 41 percent of 3rd-grade students
of color furthest from educational justice will meet standards
or higher on the ELA Smarter Balanced Assessment.*

Focusing on reading and writing is not a problem. These are foundational skills for all the other core studies and are important for life in general. I think most people would agree on the need to practice them.

The problem here is having a 41 percent pass rate as a goal, and what it tells us about the school's approach to and measurement of "learning" ELA skills. The same pass rate, 41 percent, applied to the 2022-2023 school year.

During one of our BLT meetings, we looked at the actual data collected from two of our three third-grade classrooms' Measures of Academic Progress (MAP) results. MAPs are a series of computerized adaptive tests that measure general knowledge in reading, mathematics, language usage, and science. It is one of the growth tests that schools use before their students participate in the statewide tests.

Out of twenty-nine kids, *thirteen* of them scored "average and below." If we're using that 50 percent as the pass line, then 55 percent of students passed, and 45 percent of students didn't pass. This rate remained the same for the 2021–2022 and 2022–2023 school years, as did the continual improvement priority goal.

This data was further broken down by race, with even more inequity across those lines with only 30 percent of the *"students of color furthest from educational justice"* passing.[8]

A bigger concern is that I had to be in the BLT to see these results. Parents never hear the test results—neither the raw

---

8 There are many factors that contribute to test results—missing a real learning opportunity is just one. Educational justice is a big topic that can be a book on its own, but when there isn't access to real learning for all children, it's challenging to further understand educational justice by race. We are exploring the need for real learning in this book.

numbers nor what the teachers plan to do in response. Aside from MAPs occurring twice each year, nobody even talked about it.

In theory, regular tests like MAPs do have the potential to assess and identify both the teacher's approach and how the students have responded, so that both sides can learn from each other and then figure out what will work better. But that never happened, or at least it didn't in our school.

The public school documentary *Waiting for "Superman"* explained the process further: Test scores like these have been used internally to place children on different pathways. Students with higher scores may be sent to the fast track, while kids with lower scores are put on a slower track. Again, these decisions are not discussed with students or parents.

Without changing anything on the school's side, collaborating with parents, or even communicating about the results, we can only conclude that these tests are meant to measure the children, and the children only. Seth Godin got choked up in an interview about this topic on Krista Tippet's show *On Being with Krista Tippet*. He said he is heartbroken when he hears educators say things like "Those people just can't learn."

Conclusions like this often come from test results and assessments. If all we are measuring is which kids memorized the material to score well and which did not, then the only conclusion is that some kids are better at studying than others—which the system tends to describe as "learning" better or worse—and they are treated accordingly.

But when 45 percent of third-grade children read and write at "average and below" levels, do we believe nearly half of the class can't "learn"? Shouldn't it alert us to something about the teaching and studying practices in the classroom as a whole?

Adam Grant talks about this in *Hidden Potential* as well. To bring out the best in all students, he advocates for us to "recognize that intelligence comes in many forms and every child has the potential to excel. Cultivate a growth mindset in teachers, not only in students."

A Learner's Perspective

I like my teacher and want her to like me too. But I can tell when she likes other kids better. When other kids don't like me, I play alone. When it feels like the teacher doesn't like me either, I don't even want to be there.

Rethinking Safe Environments

The more I saw behind the scenes, the more I wondered about this idea that some kids can "learn" and others can't, and how those assumptions might affect their experience at school.

Remember how I mentioned the amazing stories other parents shared about their children and their academic achievements or musical talents back in the day? I couldn't help but use these stories as a standard to look up to. I knew something was off whenever I tried to compare my children's progress against that standard. I noticed how miserable I felt whenever I did, so I stopped it. It wasn't until I started to look at what standardized testing is about that I realized comparing our children with other children is an easy trap to fall into as well.

When my kids weren't ranked at the top of their classroom, they felt less confident, and negative about their intelligence, and they questioned their ability in almost everything in life. This was especially true for my younger son. He is physically active and found his passion in competitive swimming. But since swimming ability isn't measured or valued in school, it was challenging for him to feel good about himself there. Often, when he felt low from school, he didn't even want to go to swimming practice because he wasn't sure about himself.

The only measurement the school had for its goal of a "safe and welcoming" environment was attendance. In some ways, I think a lot of parents would agree with this. I have often heard parents say, "Yes, my children like their school. Otherwise, they would refuse to go every day."

But is the school environment so safe and welcoming that simply attending is enough? My experiences in the PTA and BLT were not.

Even when we weren't discussing budget issues in the BLT, we constantly had to fend for ourselves. At one point, the power struggle between various staff representatives tipped over into bullying behaviors. It was heartbreaking and shocking to witness the people that we entrusted our children with behaving in those ways.

The parents' reaction toward the loss of the art program sent a strong message in the community that people didn't trust the school leadership team to care about students' interests and benefits. Some families left the system because they needed to find a trustworthy partner to teach their children.

Usually, we trust our schools' authority on education. We trust that our schools are watching out for our children. We trust that when our children complete their schooling and college, they will have critical thinking skills, learn how to learn, be able to work with others, do the work they enjoy and are passionate about, and live a happy life.

This trust has been the reason why many of us "get out of the schools' way," turn our heads when things go wrong, or convince ourselves that someone will figure it out.

But how can the adults in the school building create a safe and welcoming environment for our children when they aren't experiencing psychological or emotional safety among themselves?

When we don't feel safe or at ease, we do what we can to simply survive, which often includes trying to fit in or go along with a group. This was my experience of the PTA, even without the responsibility of decision-making and challenging conversations. Other parents seemed to fit in, but I later found out they felt just as out of place or even as fearful as I did.

Even if the adults in the system were able to set aside their conflicts and fears enough to welcome our children, the size of our schools alone makes it difficult to create a sense of belonging and community. Our neighborhood school has had as many as 350 children enrolled, yet it's considered one of the smaller schools in the area. The middle school and high school that my children would later be assigned to have over 1,000 students.

These are massive numbers.

In his book *The Tipping Point*, Malcolm Gladwell talked about Dunbar's number, or the law of 150. The idea is that it's possible to build a strong connection through informal personal relationships, trust, and intimacy in a group of up to 150 people that you know "well enough that what they think of you matters." Once the number grows beyond 150—in person, not online—personal connection weakens.

Gladwell used Gore Associates, the company that makes the water-resistant Gore-Tex fabric, as an example. As a billion-dollar company with thousands of employees, they diligently adhered to the law of 150 by dividing their divisions into smaller groups. By intentionally protecting a sense of community, they kept the energy and agility of a small start-up even though they were a huge international corporation.

Are our schools bringing that same intentionality to their classrooms, or do children believe that the hundreds of kids at their school are part of the same group—where "what they think of you matters"?

From all measurements, attending school does not deliver the results we expect it to, not even for the low standards that the school puts forth.

Even if we were to reduce the size of each grade or even an entire school, the challenges we face today extend far beyond size alone. The top-down school culture, rules, and regulations that enable our overgrown schools to function cohesively would still be present. When you have to push 350 kids through a list of required studying material every year while maintaining the discipline and compliance needed to maximize our school resources and meet the system's expectations—the environments that we see make sense.

But if we are seeking something beyond the efficiency of mass-produced high school graduates, then we're going to need something else. Something like the community and connection that the current environment is not built to deliver.

A Learner's Perspective

It's overwhelming to be with so many people in such a big school. I haven't made friends. I cry when I get home because I am anxious and stressed out. I feel like I don't matter.

The Gaps in Our Assumptions

My husband, Henry, was the first parent I interviewed for my podcast, Duct Tape Rocket Ship. I knew that he spent four years and tens of thousands of dollars going to college to be a mechanical engineer like his older brother, only to realize in the end that it wasn't what he wanted. But in our interview, he shared details of his story that I had never heard before then and haven't forgotten since.

This is his story.

Henry grew up in Michigan and went through the public school system all the way to college. Like many first-generation Chinese immigrants, Henry's parents were restaurant workers first, then owners. While they were busy making a living to provide for the family, they didn't have time to hang out and connect with their children. With no other relatives or friends living nearby, Henry found great comfort and validation at school. He was a "straight A" student the whole way through, took all the classes he could in high school, and got top scores on all his AP tests.

He was considered a smart, well-behaved, high-performing kid who every teacher loved to have in their classes and every parent dreamt of raising.

The news that he and a few other top-performing students had been accepted into the mechanical engineering program at Purdue University made the local newspaper. Detroit was the home to the automobile industry, where mechanical engineers were guaranteed a stable job with handsome pay. Henry would be taken care of once he graduated from college. His family was proud of him, and his future was bright.

Everything seemed to be going as planned—until he started his freshman year of college. As it turned out, engineering school was hard. Challenging work on concepts that would usually take him a year to learn was due on tight turnarounds. There just wasn't enough time. His experience of school changed so fast, so drastically, and without any warning, that he fell from cloud nine to absolute misery within three months.

There were many international students in the same classes, and Henry noticed how others seemed to plow through the material, navigating problems that had him feeling stuck. Were they that much smarter than him? He didn't think so. After working with a few kids from Hong Kong, he realized that they had already studied some of the subjects before they were accepted into the program. They seemed to also know how to navigate challenges and solve problems better than he did. He asked for help with some of his assignments, but his classmates were also pressed for time.

The gap was bigger than the help he could get.

He was in crisis both inside and out. Going from being a top student to being unable to figure out the assignments, the shift in his identity and self-narrative created even bigger challenges.

His struggle continued, and after two years he was called into the Dean's office and advised to consider other majors. Continuing engineering school would be a waste of time and money. But even with that knowledge, he stayed until senior year—not because he believed he could figure things out, but because he had never thought about what other majors he might pursue. Mechanical engineering was a guarantee for jobs and a field that his parents and family approved of and respected. Even if there were another job to consider, he had no idea what might interest him. Besides being "a top student," he never had a chance to learn what he was really good at.

Feeling alone in this deep struggle, the end of college felt like the end of all hope for success in his life. But he eventually left anyway, alone, with no degree, never to contact his college friends again.

After he moved back into his parents' house, life was just as difficult. Without much to do, he decided to go to a community college. There, he was able to explore his interests for the very first time in his life. He enrolled in an art class, where a teacher helped him uncover his interest in drawing and desire to make things beautiful. Soon after, he was accepted into a local art school and eventually became a graphic designer. His love for design was so intense that he was completely immersed in it, spending all his time in art studios for years on end.

Looking back, he said it was true that he didn't have the skills to study engineering, but it was his interest that made the difference. Because he was never really interested in engineering to begin with, he couldn't overcome the hurdles that came with it. He hadn't known what it felt like to truly love a subject, so he hadn't realized there was a problem to account for.

Despite all of this, Henry is lucky to have found his calling within five years of graduating high school. Many of us took much longer to find our passions, and some are still looking.

Meanwhile, the school's priority goals, the way the classroom environment is set up, and the way the school system measures success all point to one key assumption: if we can succeed in our studies, we will do well in everything else. But the studies are designed to squeeze children of all sizes into one box that testing scores are saying doesn't work—and even the kids who do succeed at tests aren't guaranteed to do well in life.

I call this current school environment a *studying-based* school. Everything revolves around rote studying and testing results without consideration of our individual, very human learning needs.

Studying alone doesn't connect with most people because it's not a natural way to learn. From the way a baby learns to talk to the way we adapt in our careers as adults, learning connects new information—often from trial and error—to something meaningful in our lives. Learning accelerates when we are given a variety of subjects and experiences to choose from. But more importantly, learning helps us see ourselves.

At the end of the nine-month "hands-on learning" certificate program at the local university, two-thirds of my group members had dropped out, and the remaining team presented an imaginary project that would never work in the real world. Compare that to what I have learned from Seth Godin's Akimbo Workshops, which were centered around community and learning through real-life experiences and contributed greatly to the book you are reading at this moment. Or think of my eleven-year-old son, who was struggling in school but is now on his way to becoming a chef when he grows up.

Parents need to understand the difference between studying and learning, but it's even more important for us to see the differences between the environments that support each. We've already seen what a studying environment looks like in the majority of our schools today, and how little it contributes to students' learning needs.

In the next chapter, we will take a closer look at a learning environment, and how it can support both studying and learning needs.

Chapter 5:
The Learning Environment

Studying is a collection of activities that require compliance and often have little to do with students. Learning is a process of self-connection that shows up as exploration based on interest and passion. And seeing how they aren't the same from the learners' perspective changed how I saw everything else in the school environment.

Yet even after I saw the differences between studying and learning, I found it a lot harder to identify what the learning environment is compared to studying. We can clearly point to things like rote memorization, standardized testing, grading systems, and rigid curriculum as components of a studying-based environment. But when I tried to talk about a learning environment, it wasn't as obvious.

And the reason might be simple: learning is hard to see because it happens naturally, while we are going about our everyday lives with a sense of curiosity. It shows up in millions of ways, big and small—experimenting with recipes, growing a garden, learning martial arts, improving our skills at work, trying to launch a new business, trying on clothes... You get the idea. And like Gillian Lynne, who had no problems learning as long as she got to move and dance while doing so, we all learn from these experiences in our own way.

Learning has evolved with human beings since the very beginning, long before the industrial age and the public school system that came from it. The discussions of learning in the Analects of Confucius (论语) come to mind as just one example. The Analects is an ancient Chinese book attributed to Confucius and others of his time (475–221 BC). One is "learning by metaphor" 举一反三. From understanding how one thing works, we can apply that learning somewhere else, as the Ikea owner did after his experience at the Guggenheim Museum. Another is "dripping water wears away rock" 水滴石穿 which is similar to Seth Godin's "drip by drip" teaching. This describes the importance of practice with commitment and persistence.

Human intelligence, or the ability to learn, varies widely and should be recognized, encouraged, and nurtured in all its forms—beyond the scope of academic subjects and testing alone. The environment that nurtures true learning may be difficult to pinpoint, but it is drastically different from the environment that supports studying alone.

Teaching to Learn

The internet has changed how, what, and where we can learn. Period.

Where we once benefited from gatekeepers granting us access to knowledge that we couldn't access otherwise, now we can find any information we want, delivered in any format that we need, whenever we might be interested in it. This has changed the responsibility of the teacher from delivering information to finding ways to make the information resonate with students so they can absorb it.

But before we dive into the details of learning and environment, there is "enrollment" to consider. Instead of thinking of enrollment as the physical applications to fill out, it is about taking ownership of one's learning because you want to do it.

I joined a Creatives workshop at Akimbo[9]—an adult learning space founded by Seth Godin in 2015 to "help people learn to see," which I interpret to mean seeing beyond what's obvious. The lessons were presented in almost any format you could imagine: video recordings, YouTube clips, drawings, songs, articles, cartoons, interviews, etc. The point was to get information and ideas across through engaging and effective mediums so

---

9 Seth Godin passed Akimbo workshops to fellow founding members in early 2020. https://www.akimbo.com/about

that many learning styles could follow along. After each lesson, there were prompts to help us think about the lesson and articulate our takeaways.

One of my favorite lessons in the Creatives workshop talked directly about the process of learning. It was an interview between Seth Godin and Gabe Anderson, a bass player in Nashville who writes daily blog posts about culture and music.

What stood out to me in their conversation was the topic of internalization. Gabe noticed that great musicians create work that resonates with themselves to the point that the art works for others as well. Seth elaborated on this by explaining that, when artists internalize enough of genre and culture, they are doing the work for other people—even when they don't feel that way. Good work, generous work, is work that resonates and connects with audiences.

The same applies to any learning environment: good teaching that makes our children better provides choices, channels, and mediums that resonate and connect with them. Learning that resonates enables integration and internalization that studying can't, for many.

In this short, seventeen-minute interview, they also talked about the differences between gifts and skills, and how changing our point of view around them changes our collective view about ourselves and each other. They explained that we need new skills to do better work—not gifts or talent—and since skills can be learned, there is no reason for anyone to believe that we can't improve. In other words, there's no one who "can't learn," as schools sometimes decide for our children.

The Creatives Workshop, with the goal of supporting people through their creative process, helped us learn skills in a way that resonated, so we could do our work in the world. Everyone came up with a project they wanted to work on, and the lessons conveyed important ideas and perspectives that we could integrate into that project. Our focus was on a self-defined goal we had set out to achieve, and learning was contextualized by that project. There were no tests or grades at the end or along the way. There was no falling behind. The only tension we had was the time we had in the workshop with one another, but how we made the most of it was up to us.

This model is called project-based learning. While it looks different from the K-12 schools to adult learning spaces because of developmental needs and skill requirements, it works on the same principles and produces similar results in any dynamic. Because of its effectiveness, and because it is a teaching model that closely follows our natural ways of learning, this model is going to be my primary example of a learning environment for the rest of this book—Akimbo as the adult learning example, and Summit Public Schools as the middle and high school example.

Project-based Learning

Seth Godin created a close-knit community in the workshops within Akimbo, one that was more than just the concept of community that I had experienced in schools. The teachers and coaches acted as guides instead of authorities. Support and feedback mostly came from peers generously contributing to other people's learning, allowing us to accept help and support from others as well.

Through his understanding of various learning needs, the effectiveness of the network, the value and belief in generosity—giving is more important than taking, and with the power of positive peer pressure, participants felt like we were all in the experience of learning together, and more importantly, learning in the real sense of community.

In workshops like these—online, project-based learning spaces for adults—the presence of teachers is not necessary. The content does the heavy lifting of teaching, and learning occurs as we apply the teaching to our projects. Coaches only step in when students need feedback or have questions. The rest of the work is up to us and our peers.

Project-based learning in a school setting looks different but is based on a similar concept. When my older son graduated from our neighborhood public school at age eleven, we moved him to a local public charter school called Summit Public Schools, which is known for their project-based learning. In Summit, everything is in the project format, with two kinds of projects—studying projects and learning projects.[10]

Studying projects are foundational subjects such as literature, math, history, etc. They are taught as classes that students are required to attend for the majority of the school year, but they are tracked in a project format. Because students don't have a choice with these mandatory, graded projects, we call them **studying** projects. But even with these studying projects, kids have the autonomy to choose which area they want to focus on first within each project, and self-pace for completion—some students finish the project fast, while others take their time to complete given the same project start and end date.

These projects are designed to cover grade-appropriate studying points as the student completes the assessment components built into the projects. Each project builds on the previous one to facilitate incremental growth and results. At the end of each project, instead of a test, the final product demonstrates what they have understood. For example, a final product can be a choice between a podcast that includes several two to five-minute-long episodes about 'a good life' and an essay about what makes life good. This studying format further encourages choice and exploration.

---

10 The Summit Learning Platform is demonstrated here:
https://help.summitlearning.org/hc/en-us/
articles/227078348-Logging-into-the-Summit-Learning-platform

Because these schools weren't built around grades to rank or label kids, students have opportunities to improve their studying projects for higher grades. After all, the real measurement isn't the grade but how much they understood and absorbed from their projects, as well as their incremental growth over time.

Summit's **learning** projects are called Expedition, and they are available from sixth grade up to the twelfth grade. For the 2022–2023 school year, each student had nine weeks out of the school year dedicated to these learning projects.[11] Every year, each student gets to choose from more than thirty projects in categories like fashion design, performing arts, martial arts, Lego robotics, murals, concept art, music production, wilderness science, swimming, applied mechanics, gaming, machine learning, AI, etc. If students don't see their interests on the list, they are encouraged to propose their own ideas, and school-assigned mentors will work with them to develop their unique projects. While these learning projects are required for participation, they are not graded or assessed. They don't even show up on the report cards. Period. These are important distinctions between the learning projects at Summit versus the Music and Art programs at our neighborhood public school.

Expedition isn't an after-school enrichment program or interest club. Like studying projects, learning projects take place on school days led by well trusted and respected local specialists and entrepreneurs. This makes the program beyond remarkable—*every* student gets to participate in a way that helps them embrace learning. Individual choice sets students up for maximum motivation, ownership, and personal commitment from the very start of the school year.

---

11 The nine weeks were grouped into five learning project cycles with two weeks per cycle, except for the last cycle that only has one week. The entire school year is a rotation between studying projects and the learning projects, which goes like this: six weeks of studying projects (math, literature, science etc.) followed by two weeks of learning projects. And just like studying projects, learning projects are pursued during school days.

At school, each student has a mentor who stays with them through the entirety of their middle school years and another mentor for all their high school years. Mentors and students meet weekly to share and reflect on their studying and learning. When a student is stuck on a homework assignment for any reason, their subject teachers, mentors, and peers are there to help them get unstuck. Mentors serve as long-term coaches for the children, building trust and understanding as they guide students over time, instead of serving as one-year authorities, like at our neighborhood school.

A Learner's Perspective

When we have the opportunity to learn and choose, we are more willing to embark on the journey, commit to it, and reach our own goals at the finish line.
Learning is vulnerable, especially when we are feeling stuck. Having the same mentor or coach in our corner over a long period is a much-needed support that truly makes a difference in our practice and learning.

The Role of Peers

A learning environment cannot be effective without peer support and positive peer pressure. Peers are the people who choose to be on the same journey in the same learning space, sharing similar interests and goals. In the adult learning environment, peer support often turns into friendships that last for a lifetime. Through our shared experience and values, we learn more about each other, connect deeply, and contribute to each other's learning and growth.

That makes connection-building the first step in a cohort. In order to offer each other helpful feedback, we need to know more about each other: where we came from, where we are now, and where we wish to go. Alone, we can be taught concepts, spot some differences, and find new ways to see people and the work we do. But if we want to learn about our audience's perspective, learn different ways of seeing things, learn from other people's responses toward our project, and most importantly, hear honest feedback, we must learn from our peers.

After we moved Sebastian to Summit, I asked how he felt about other children in the school. He shared something he observed as unique to Summit: In Expedition, kids are way more willing to connect and help each other. I wasn't surprised to hear that but happy to see the change that learning has brought into their school community. Was it because the shared interest and passion brought students closer to each other with connection and a sense of camaraderie? Was it because no grading meant less competition but more cooperation and sharing? Was it because enrollment and connection inspire kids to give more than take (like generosity in the Creatives Workshop)? This observation told me something important about learning and the learning environment.

Another observation he had was that everyone is equal there. When I asked him what that meant, he told me that at our neighborhood public school, children were treated differently, and favoritisms were often in play. Some of the children were preferred over the rest of the kids. Not just within peer groups, but from the adults as well. And that it hurt.

Now, when I pick up Sebastian from Summit, he is relaxed, calm, and happy. This is a huge shift from the grumpy, frustrated, and impatient kid he had become in school before we moved him.

A studying environment is about individual achievement, centered on grades and pass rates, while a learning environment is centered on individual learning paths and exploration. This change alleviates the pressure of competition but promotes collaboration in nature. An effective learning environment is one where everyone's individual dream is accepted and respected as equal. We are fellow travelers who are willing to partner with and support each other regardless of our identities, backgrounds, experiences, or job titles. We notice our differences, but we also see our sameness on a deeper level. When the environment allows, we are more eager to contribute to each other's journey, and that makes peer-supported learning more connected and effective.

A Learner's Perspective

Acceptance goes both ways. When we are accepted as who we are and what we dream to be, we accept others as their whole, true selves as well.

The Role of Teachers

Creating a resonant, group-supported learning environment isn't about entertaining the students. Being interesting is important, but the quality of teaching is what makes the difference.

Summit Public Schools understands students' individuation and the difference that choice brings in a school environment. They maximize choices in everything that students do, from self-pacing and prioritizing studying projects to full choice autonomy in Expedition. Mentors (classroom teachers) support students every step of the way by meeting students at their level and working with them to make incremental growth without lower expectations from everyone.

At Akimbo, Seth Godin has deep empathy and understanding for the creatives who join these workshops. He knows their challenges and what it is like to be creative in a world where success is largely defined by status and money. He believes in the importance of curiosity and creative work, doing better work to fight the mediocrity of "race to the bottom" models, and solving problems through learning. He also understands our learning experiences, challenges, and the need for engagement within teaching moments.

Within his workshops, Seth's material is always practical and insightful. And since we own the teaching content within the workshop, we get to watch it over and over, at our own timing and pace. The different mediums he includes simply expand the learning experiences he is creating for us.

When a teaching focus shifts from lengthy lectures to resonance and connection, it doesn't eliminate a teaching job. Instead, it opens up strategic options and deepens the impact and results of teaching. Students are more willing to lean in because of interesting and provoking content. One example from Akimbo is to have students listen to Lin-Manuel Miranda's interview about his experience writing "My Shot" for *Hamilton*. What can students learn about genre and originality? Guiding students to share through a discussion leads to a much deeper internalization of what they are learning.

A Learner's Perspective

When we experience this level of understanding, care, trust, and empathy, we take our learning and the work more seriously. When we feel that we are understood and cared for, we are more willing to trust both the learning environment and ourselves. When we are accepted for who we are and were born to be, we feel validated by ourselves and the people around us. We are more willing to accept and support others for who they are.

The Importance of Choice

Adam Grant explained in *Hidden Potential*, "Extensive evidence shows that the wellspring of intrinsic motivation is having the freedom of opportunity to explore our interests."

Choice is an important way to identify learning environments.

When I was in the university certificate program, the school presented something in project format, also known as 'hands-on learning.' This is often paired with the concept of "real-world experience." But instead of choosing our projects based on what mattered to us, we were given five predefined projects and asked to form teams. Eventually, what we would do and how we would do it became a team decision. If we insisted on doing a project that was out of scope, which already required us to stand out from the norm, it wasn't encouraged. We would be working alone. Hence, nobody was willing to try.

This is not the same thing as project-based learning.

When I first joined Akimbo, shortly after the university program, the biggest difference I noticed was how different it felt to create or present my own project as part of the learning process. At first, it was overwhelming. In the traditional, studying-centered environment, students rarely get to learn about themselves, let alone choose what they want to learn. I had many projects in my head, and I simply didn't know which one to pick.

I joined because I knew that I needed to develop skills, confidence, and trust in myself to move forward on my creative journey. I had no idea what we were going to do or learn. But I also quickly realized that I wasn't alone in feeling this way. And that was OK. Once I understood the cohort, the intention of the workshop, and the projects I had on my plate, I was able to choose what I wanted to focus on and then see it through to the end of the workshop.

Project-based learning can be centered on a person's passion, interests, or a choice of intriguing problems to solve. If you want to write a book, you may choose to learn the creative process by figuring out a writing practice, genre, point of view, and idiosyncrasy. The same goes for drawing, making a song, or exploring nature—your project might be centered around a painting, blog, newsletter, creative process for music, marketing campaign, etc.

Or you can choose to solve a problem: design a better journal, meet a specific need around website design, or build an app for kids who need mental health support.

Many people think this kind of luxury is only available to the adult learning world, but Summit's example tells us that it's possible to offer choice and learning in all schools.

Interaction with Peers

Project-based learning combines individual choice with a cohort setting. To understand that fully, we first need to understand one more component of a learning environment compared to a studying environment.

Using our neighborhood school during COVID as an example, the model of teaching and studying is executed from the top down. We might visualize it as a triangle, where information moves from the teacher presenting the material to the students who are listening as best they can, and then the students send their studying assignments back to the teacher for approval.

A cohort model, where project-based learning happens, is more like a circle. Students depend on and support each other as they go, giving each other feedback as everyone integrates the learning. Throughout this process, mentors and teachers support each student at both individual and cohort levels.

For schools, the studying-centered environment often emphasizes individual excellence. Achievement is often credited back to individual efforts, perseverance, and commitment.

This is the opposite of a learning environment, where every child's learning is included and valued. Learning-centered schools like Summit value both individual excellence as well as the well-being of the community. Supporting one another isn't just a job for mentors, teachers, and leaders, but peers as well. Students need to have both intentional directions from the teachers as well as peer guidance around how they want to participate and interact with one another, and it is possible to strike a balance between both.

Measurement and Progress

Washington state requires compulsory testing, which Summit participates in. But the connection, integration, and internalization of knowledge don't happen because someone sets a date by which they should be absorbed. It doesn't happen because someone asks all students to progress the same way. Learning and studying happen because students make a connection to things that sparked their interest and curiosity, and motivated them to move forward.

The built-in assessment components throughout each studying project are an important way to help students, mentors, and teachers stay on track with individualized studying paths. Incremental gap closure and small progress contribute to much bigger growth and results over time, without lowering expectations for every student.

For parents who worry that their students might not be able to perform in college entrance tests or do well in studying-centered schools later on, Summit Public Schools have published their results from within a project-based model: 96 percent of Summit graduates are accepted to four-year colleges, including both public and private universities and colleges, and Summit alumni go on to complete college at two times the rate of the US national average.

I have witnessed this success anecdotally, as well. You already know that when Sebastian was in our neighborhood elementary school, his reading and writing scores were always slightly below grade level. Within three rounds of Expedition

The Hierarchy Model

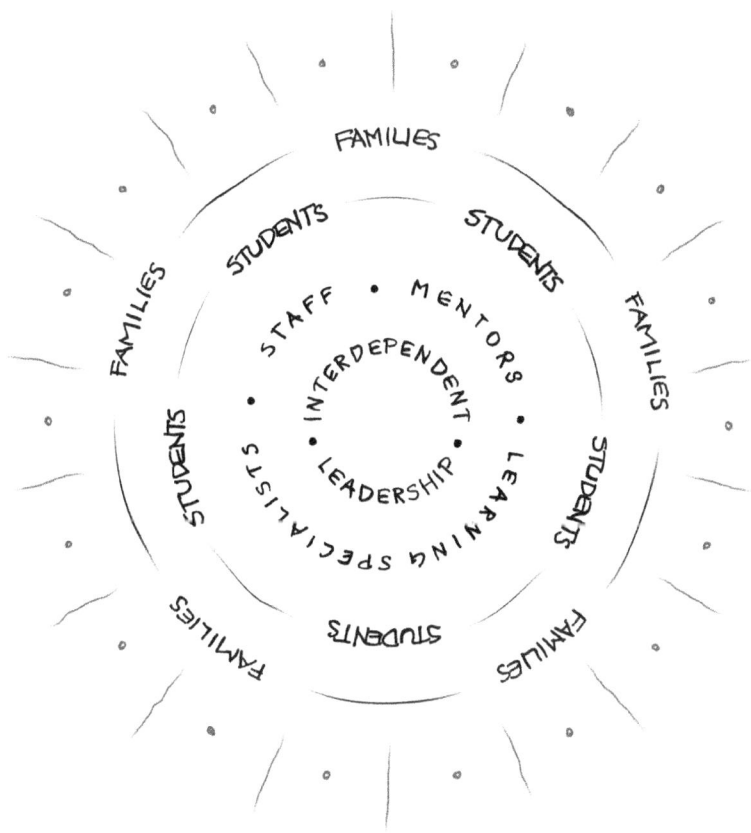

The Interdependence Model

programs at Summit—six projects and six weeks of exploring, experimenting, and learning—not only did he catch up to the grade level but also advanced his study.

Projects connected him to different learning disciplines and a range of subjects that allowed integration and internalization to happen. This, not rigid studying and testing routines, contributed to a measurable outcome.

A Chance to Dream

From my experiences within the Creatives workshops, I have learned:

Learning is not a competition. Everyone has their own pace and goals to reach.

Learning doesn't always look like success. We learn from trial and error, which means we must also learn how to quit. There were times when the project we chose to work on didn't work out, so we got to choose whether to stick to it and make it work, or give it up and start a new one.

Learning has no hidden secrets. It's about practice, skills, commitment, and showing up.

Akimbo workshops are not teaching to a test or grades—because the goal is to learn. Individual interests and self-paced integration guide, and neither would be measured well through testing.

Project-based learning is rooted in the belief that individuals have an innate curiosity and desire to learn and create, and this belief allows us to progress at our own pace. It also leads us to trust our own thoughts, skills, and points of view.

Even though the project-based learning at Summit looks different from Akimbo Workshops because of the developmental need and skill requirement differences between children and adults, the goal of Summit Public Schools is to help every student lead a fulfilled life after finishing their education. It's nearly impossible to have a fulfilled life if children don't have a dream, don't know what they are interested in, or never have a chance to do something about those interests.

It's nearly impossible to have a fulfilled life if they are bullied into medical school but can't sustain the career and leave the field, for instance, or are sent to follow a family's definition of success while constantly struggling with self-acceptance. It's nearly impossible to have a fulfilled life if the only reason to go to college is to get a job they have no interest in doing.

The ultimate purpose of project-based learning is to prepare students with the skills and confidence it takes to thrive in the world—a world, it's worth noting, that is without tests.

As a kid, I was often asked, "What do you want to become when you grow up?" I rarely hear people ask my kids this nowadays. COVID turned our attention back to purpose—life purpose, work purpose, team purpose, etc. But we're still learning to talk about our dreams. In a project-based learning community, every project that students choose to do takes them one step closer to their dreams.

When interviewing clients for their brand strategy, Henry and I ask, "If money weren't an issue and you could have any business you want in the whole world, what would that be?" I love this question because I love dreams. I love this question because it gives people permission and freedom to dream, even just for a moment. I love this question because when I see a smile from the client before they answer, I know that we have begun to form a connection.

My sixth grader dreams of becoming a chef when he grows up, and he has turned this dream into his learning goals and the guide for his projects. As part of the encouragement for every student to both dream and be proud of their dreams, they make a presentation for their family members about their goals and ambitions. Then they make them known to friends, peers, mentors, and people they care about who also care about them.

Because of my son's dream, he has a clear understanding of why he needs to study subjects like science, reading, writing, math, history, etc., and how studying those subjects helps him learn what he needs to know to become a chef. His dream and learning at Summit have unlocked his motivation and emotional enrollment with his studying. This is the profound and remarkable change I saw happen in him, and for that, I am forever grateful.

Without the opportunity to dream, students are stuck in a dark corner wondering what the point of school is at all. Why do I need to do the homework? Why is it important to practice reading and writing? What's the point of studying?

I would ask the same questions if I were in their shoes.

A Learner's Perspective

When I don't know how something is going to help me to do the things that I really care about or could imagine doing, it's painful to comply. But when I understand how studying and learning connect to my dreams and life goals, I am willing to participate and commit with my own purpose in mind.

Chapter 6:
Who Is School For?

Losing the art program sent parents into an outrage—but not all for the same reasons. For some, the problem wasn't even that the program was gone, but that the school had not asked for the parents' thoughts before they made the decision. The decision had apparently been made among the PTA, alongside the Building Leadership Team (BLT). Meanwhile, others didn't see the loss as a big deal at all. Why worry about something so unimportant, especially when volunteers could help children draw and paint?

Among the mixed emotions that arose at that time, the one most overlooked and often misunderstood was, "My kids love art and are so upset about losing the program."

Much later, after I noticed the differences between studying and learning, I saw the entire situation in a new light. An art program is one of the few opportunities closest to learning that our children have in a studying-centric school system. Children who are not connected to the studying subjects (reading, writing, and math) naturally tend to connect to their preferred subjects. Some to art, some to music, some to PE, and some to other subjects beyond the school's availability.

In a project-based learning environment like Summit's Expedition, art and music are included in project options that students can choose from. They might decide to create a mural, develop a music production, or center their project on dance, a sport, or martial arts.

In our neighborhood school, the parents of children who didn't connect with art didn't see the problem in losing the art program, and the system didn't see the problem as a priority. After all, success is solely measured by test outcomes, not what kids connect to or not.

But the kids who connected with art weren't just losing a fun program. They were losing their access to a program that was closest to learning.

One of the responsibilities I felt I had as the parent representative in the BLT was to work with the team and the PTA to build a parent feedback channel so the school could make the best decisions possible for the community. I didn't realize that listening to all the parents would be such a challenge.

Often, parents who are passionate about advocating for our children do so because we hope it will help them do well in school. We want everyone in the school to know that we have worries, concerns, and suggestions. And, more importantly, we want our voices to be heard.

For many parents, speaking up and being known as part of the PTA is considered the safest route for that advocacy. Because of its history and its role in the public school system, the PTA has a system in place to provide learning opportunities for parents, surveys of the community's needs, and data collection that could be presented to the Building Leadership Team for the decision-making process.

What I learned from this experience helped me realize that the membership count of the PTA, about 10 percent of the total parent population at our local school between 2020 to 2023, isn't broad enough to represent everyone. When the rest of the parents weren't heard and represented, they were the voices that had been left out.

This brings up a very serious question that we rarely stop to ask; we don't usually question who the public school system was made for.

Everyone Is Welcome!

It was about a year from the first time I received a flyer through the mail saying *"Everyone is welcome! We need your help!"* to the moment I decided to look into the PTA. As a species, we humans join in with others because we don't want to stand alone or feel lonely. So of course, it's intriguing to think there's a group that would welcome you. What held me back was that the messages, both verbal and non-verbal, that I received from the PTA were confusing.

From the beginning, the welcome from people in the school felt less than warm. Okay, there is a difference between being polite and being welcoming. We feel it. As someone once said, energy never lies. Non-verbal cues are often more important than verbal ones, and unlike the messages communicated in fliers and requests, the school environment felt distant and was even hostile at times. With such mixed messaging, cues, and feelings, I started to wonder if it was just me. But then I would walk into a real community, like a neighborhood gym, and the truly warm welcome from everyone there would make me question my experience in our school yet again.

As we approached the end of the kindergarten year, I wondered if the feeling of not belonging was simply because I wasn't a PTA member. Even though my husband and I attended school auctions and donated, we had never attended the PTA meetings. Maybe that was why I felt out of place. Maybe I would feel different if I joined the PTA. I was hopeful.

When I walked into a PTA meeting for the first time, things became clear. Fast.

I arrived at the cafeteria right before the meeting started. Several volunteers were hanging around at the door, and they all looked surprised to see me. Nobody said anything as I approached. No greeting. No questions. No check-in. Nothing. I hesitated at the door, wondering if I should check in, then two more people headed over to the doors and began to close them. Feeling a little awkward, I decided to just walk in.

Parents were sitting at long lunch tables facing the doors, and there was another small table and a podium for the host and guest speakers. I walked past everyone to find a seat and landed in an empty one all the way in the back. The first familiar face appeared when the meeting started—the host was a parent from the same classroom as me. That was at least a little relief since I didn't know anybody else in the room.

Near the end of the meeting, the host asked people to vote. But I didn't hear what she said exactly. Raising my hand to ask a question felt risky in this already awkward situation. I wasn't sure what to do, and quickly went into panic mode. My instincts told me it would be a bad idea to draw attention to myself at this moment. So when the others' hands went up, I raised my hand as well. Doing what the others did felt safe, even though I had no idea what I was doing.

The host counted hands row by row. But when her eyes met mine and she saw my hand, she stopped counting and skipped to the next person sitting on the other side of the aisle. I couldn't help but feel embarrassed and stupid. Luckily, nobody seemed to notice, but I was angry with myself. Why did I do that?!

The minute the meeting ended, I walked out as fast as I could. Clearly, the PTA was not meant for people like me. I had no idea how else to think about the situation or to turn things around in my mind.

If the PTA were people like me, why it didn't feel that way?

If there were others out there who felt like I did, where *would* we belong in school?

Yet feeling out of place somehow propelled me to want to help the school even more. If I felt that way in the school environment, did my children and maybe others feel the same?

Who Are We Volunteering For?

If we constantly have negative experiences when being ourselves, it's nearly impossible to feel safe, let alone find a sense of belonging, and certainly not a mutual concern for welfare. And the PTA dynamics are not the only challenge. At our neighborhood school at least, there is usually a rewards system inside of the classrooms. When children follow the rules and uphold behavioral expectations, the teacher rewards them for having remarkable behavior.

In our first grader's classroom, there was a reward called "having lunch with Ms. M." When children followed Ms. M's request and met her expectations, they got to sit with her during lunchtime. It was an honor that six-year-olds competed for.

In the lower grades, personal goals in the classroom were also rewarded, such as the number of sight words and reading goals children were given for the end of the year. Neither of my children achieved their goals in this kind of environment.

Rewards systems aren't a problem, but how kids are rewarded is the question. When the rewards system is centered on compliance and unhelpful status, it invites favoritism. Giving a child verbal praise after standing up for a friend who was being bullied is very different from mentioning a child's name over and over simply because her mom volunteered that day or for what his dad had done for the teachers.

Whether we want to admit it, that kind of special treatment happens often, and makes me wonder who the rewards are really for—the child's motivation or the parent's satisfaction? And in the same light, who are we volunteering for? Do our kids have to have us there, or do we hope to appease the system so that our children are given special treatment in return?

Who Is the PTA For?

As parents, we all want the same thing: the peace of mind that our children are taken care of. We volunteer because we want to help our children learn and grow. We want them to learn about themselves and the world, find joy and love, solve problems, make friends, dream and make those dreams come true, become members who contribute to society and live their lives to the fullest.

We want to make their potential a reality, so we volunteer where we can and advocate when we must.

On the National PTA website, the mission statement says this: "PTA's mission is to make every child's potential a reality by engaging and empowering families and communities to advocate for all children." This sounds just as appealing as "Everyone Is Welcome." Based on that mission, listening to parents' worries and concerns should inform the PTA on how school services can improve. In the case of the art program, for example, surveying the community through online questionnaires, phone calls, personal conversations, and even paperwork through 'kids mail' could have helped the organization understand what they didn't know and couldn't see.

Sounds simple, right? However, a survey requires partnership and insights from many people. And in the public school system, only the school and the PTA are allowed to access a student's family's contact information. If a parent representative in the BLT plans to survey the entire parent group, they either have to partner with the rest of the BLT or engage the PTA to distribute the online or paper survey. It's nearly impossible to survey all the parents without this support.

Convincing the PTA to do the survey didn't lead to much success. In my second year at the Building Leadership Team, the principal of the school, also a BLT member, approved the project, and the survey was sent out to all the parents. Finally.

Meanwhile, whenever the BLT needed to make decisions or the parent representative needed to consult parents, the only people that I could consult with at the PTA were the two members at the top. Nobody else was invited by the PTA leaders to the meeting to share their thoughts. I was starting to see how easy it had been to decide on the art program between just two people.

I couldn't help but wonder, who is the PTA really for?

Who Is the BLT For?

Most of the time, the parent representative's role in the BLT is to learn the system and understand how it operates. There are two reasons for this. First of all, parents are not often familiar with the system's protocols, coded languages, and procedures required to understand most of the discussions that happen among teachers, staff members, and the principal. Participation is only possible when we understand how it operates. Second, very few parents in the BLT want to disagree with the other members of the team, because the stakes are too high—the potential for backlash and retaliation feel so real. No matter how hard we try, there is unequal footing among the BLT members from the start.

Advocating for children from within the public school system is stressful and anxiety-inducing. The increasing budget struggles in school meant there aren't enough resources for everyone, yet we still need to fight for children. These anxieties and stressors come from a misalignment between what we know about our children and what the school system is doing. For example, you know that your child connects to the art program and thrives on learning through art, but the art program is the least-valued subject and is let go every time there is a budget cut. We want to advocate for kids and what they need, but many of us are constantly worried about offending someone by asking for something we shouldn't.

The current school system values studying and believes it is the only way to develop and measure human intelligence. So, for parents whose children's intelligence thrives in learning environments such as art, dance, music, gaming, sports, etc.—we already know their needs will be the least recognized or valued by the school system. Until we can agree on a more helpful way to view human intelligence *or* learn how to articulate this misalignment, the stress is here to stay.

When we finally sent around our survey, parents shared their thoughts and concerns in a way that helped the BLT understand their voices.

More than 64 percent of the students in our school came from families of color. The online survey was inaccessible for nearly 100 percent of these kids and their families. Based on this knowledge, the BLT adapted different survey methods, reaching out to people we knew through email and phone calls. This personal contact survey often generated a nearly 100 percent response rate, but at the same time, it was biased toward our personal preferences and our ability to reach out to people we already had a relationship with. Having multiple team members conduct the survey would have helped with the bias issue as well as with finding additional patterns.

About seventy-five percent of parents who were surveyed supported the art program to stay—the voice of the parents was clear and straightforward. The sensible decision for the BLT would be to split the resources equally between art and music, as many other schools would do. But it didn't happen that way. The music teacher needed a full-time job, and with higher seniority, the school wasn't willing to lose that teacher by reducing the music program to a part-time position. The art teacher was willing to leave and not come back again, and this decision was applauded by many other teachers as a practice of respecting seniority (again, this book isn't about finding individuals to blame but to understand the system as a whole).

There is tremendous pressure for parents who work in the BLT alongside teachers, staff, and the principal, especially in a situation like this. I couldn't help but disagree. As much as I understood their reasons, these questions remained with me: What about the children? When the school makes a decision that's contrary to what the students connect to, are we a teacher/administration-centered school?

Who is the BLT really for?

Who Is the System For?

Parents who were familiar with the system knew exactly who to reach out to when our kids lost the art program: the school district board of directors, legislators, and the district superintendent. After months of Zoom meetings, phone calls, emails, and conversations, the final verdict from the superintendent was this: letting the art program go was the decision made by the school Building Leadership Team (BLT), and parents should talk to the BLT for resolutions. There was nothing further to be done about the art program.

With the BLT and PTA so clearly becoming the main channels for advocacy, parents looking for a way to learn about and contribute to the system turn to volunteering in those spaces. But from what I observed, many people—including parents—believe that the parents' input doesn't matter in the Building Leadership Team.

The BLT has its own agenda to push, and there is hardly any flexibility to alter it. The system isn't open to different ideas and thoughts. Additionally, not many school staff members realize or seem to care that we, the parents, are customers of the public school system. Parents have the buying power. We get to choose what kind of school we align with. The decline in public school enrollment since the pandemic has proven that parents are exercising this power by choosing other options such as private schools and homeschooling.

If we want to be our true selves as parents *and* stay in the public school system, it will include disagreeing with teachers, staff, or the principal. Some of them understand and respond with empathy; some will take it personally and respond by lashing out at our kids. This makes it difficult to show up fully with our thoughts, perspectives, and advocacy.

There is no additional protection from the system towards parent representatives and our children. The public school system treats the parent representative the same as regular parents in the school, regardless of the potential risks may incur by working so closely with teachers and staff.

After two years in the BLT, I understood why the parent representative position was wide open and nobody, especially members of the PTA, was willing to fill it. When parents did join, they often agreed with people who held more power instead of staying focused on the real priority: speaking up for the children.

The system is intricate, and very few of those pieces seem to be made for our kids.

Who Is a Learning Environment For?

In a learning environment like Summit Public Schools, parent involvement takes on a whole different dynamic. Inside the school itself, parents are only needed when students share their personal learning plan for the year with the mentor and the parents together. Since the most effective way to connect children with their interests and passions is through their dreams and who they want to become when they grow up, the kids are encouraged to shape their projects around that vision and then share their plans.

Understanding our children and supporting them as they chase their dreams is the most important role parents and caregivers have, so these schools bring parents on board with the long-term goals the children create for themselves. This is the only real need for parents to get involved.

Using my son as an example, he stated his dream and this North Star guided his studying and project choices during the school year. After he presented his personal learning plan to us and his mentor, we became a team that could support his work toward his goal for the year.

Because our children are accepted for who they are and connected with their dreams for life and goals for the year, everyone on the team is clear about what we are working toward and why we are doing what we are doing. We are not anxious about what someone else might prioritize, whether our advocacy in one area might jeopardize another, or whether our children will have to do things simply to comply without understanding why they are doing them.

The truth is, all school environments should be learning environments.

When the purpose of the school, the learning environment, the students, and the parents are all aligned, we see cohesion and efficiency at all levels without ongoing conflict, power struggles, or danger of disagreement. The school and students do what they wholeheartedly want to do, and parents support them wholeheartedly as well. Parents have more peace of mind and less stress about wanting help and contribute all the time to gain favor or a chance at being heard. A peaceful, calm school community is a demonstration of real safety and trust, and an effective way to bring peace of mind and assurance to parents leaving our children in the school's hands.

There is no doubt that parents need and should advocate for our children and support their schools, but what we are most concerned about is our children's learning needs and how we might help the school meet them.

Many parents volunteer just to be seen by the system and hopefully make sure our children are doing well. But years of volunteering at our neighborhood school didn't resolve our concerns.

Working with the PTA didn't resolve our concerns.

Maybe school as we know it wasn't about meeting every child's learning needs. And in that case, maybe parents volunteer at school for something else—something we can call the "status game."

Chapter 7:
The Status Game

A playground at a park is very different from a playground at a school. I learned this when my children were young. On the preschool playground, everyone is connected in one way or another, and kids tend to be more considerate toward each other. But outside of those boundaries, things change.

One cloudy day, I decided to take my four-year-old to a bigger playground at a park where there were many options for him to choose from. After he spent some time on the slides, he moved onto a big merry-go-round with rails all around the edges. Four other children were there playing—running, pushing it in circles, and laughing. He waited for them to stop, slow down, and maybe invite him on to the equipment. Instead, one of the girls told him, "You can't play here." A boy chimed in, "Go away!"

My son didn't move, but the other children were determined to exclude him. The situation got serious, fast. Not only was he not invited to join them, but they wanted him to go away so he wouldn't "get them in trouble." Maybe they had done the same thing before and received a negative consequence from their own parents or the parents of the excluded children. I wouldn't know. The unpleasant memory urged them to avoid the potential threat of punishment, but not to make a different choice. My son wasn't a new friend they could meet instead of exclude—he represented a potential "threat," simply by standing there, and they had to get rid of him by any means necessary.

Exclusivity is nothing new. Vivian Paley, an American preschool and kindergarten teacher and early childhood education researcher, addressed this issue in her own way in her kindergarten classroom decades ago. She noticed the ways young children use their verbal power to reject other kids, especially when a game had already started, so she decided to impose a new rule: "You can't say 'You can't play.'"

Children tend to have preferences for some of their peers and not others, as we all do, but exclusivity is about more than just friendship. It's about accessibility of play and mutual acceptance. She was asking her students to change their attitudes and expectations toward the other children who, for whatever reasons, were not yet part of their system. She was changing what would be accepted as normal in her classroom.

In her book, *You Can't Say You Can't Play*, she explained that children who experienced a negative emotional impact from being socially excluded would experience a negative impact in studying as well, because the emotional impact is too strong for kids to pay attention in class.

Years before, Jane Elliott had come to the same conclusion, covered by the PBS documentary, "A Class Divided." The day after Martin Luther King, Jr. was murdered, she divided her all-white, third-grade class into blue-eyed and brown-eyed groups. Instead of teaching children to imagine what it was like for people who were discriminated against, she taught them what it was like to actually live with discrimination.

On the first day of the experience, the blue-eyed group was placed on top of the social hierarchy, and the brown-eyed group was given that status on day two. By the end of the lesson, all of the children in her classroom had been both accepted and praised and discriminated against and excluded. It was an important lesson for the children, but it also taught educators something important. Here's what Jane had to say about her findings:

"The second year I did this exercise, I gave little spelling tests, math tests, and reading tests two weeks before the exercise, each day of the exercise, and two weeks later. And, almost without exception, the students' scores go up on the day they're on the top (socially), down on the day they're on the bottom,

and then maintain a higher level for the rest of the year after they've been through the exercise. We sent some of those tests to Stanford University to the Psychology Department and they did sort of an informal review of them. They said that what's happening here is kids' academic ability is being changed in a 24-hour period. And it isn't possible, but it's happening. Something very strange is happening to these children because suddenly they're finding out how really great they are, and they are responding to what they know now they are able to do. And it's happened consistently with third graders."

We might not need science to understand the simple truth about this outcome: we have the most capacity to learn, grow, and thrive when we are cared for, loved, nurtured, and feel great about being ourselves.

What many parents don't realize is that these are the exact same needs that drive us to play the status game.

Understanding Status

Classrooms typically reflect the culture, values, and beliefs of the surrounding society. When those dynamics no longer serve the goal of learning, schools have a choice to overwrite them. (That is, of course, if a school's purpose is to serve all children on their learning journey, which we've seen is not always the case.)

Vivian Paley and Jane Elliott's stories have three important things in common:

1. It's possible to create a separate classroom culture that's different from the dominant societal culture.

2. Accessibility and acceptance—two main barriers to closing gaps in status—can both be changed to create more equality and support for students than we thought possible.

3. Status affects studying and learning outcomes.

Status exists in everything we do. The word "status" has a fairly unproblematic source:

*stā-, *Proto-Indo-European root meaning "to stand, set down, make or be firm," with derivatives meaning "place or thing that is standing."*[12]

But over time, it has come to be measured in comparison to others. According to wiktionary.org, status is:

a person's condition, position, or standing relative to that of others (in the society).[13]

If we piece together definitions of both *status* and *game,* we get:

A status game is an attempt to elevate one's condition, position, or standing relative to that of others through a structured form of "play," according to rules and decided by skill, strength, luck, or manipulation.

Loretta Graziano Breuning explores this dynamic in her book, *Status Games: Why We Play and How to Stop.* She says that human brains alarm us about danger and threats with the hormone cortisol and generate happy feelings through serotonin. We feel good (serotonin) when we are in a higher status and bad (with cortisol, the stress hormone) when we are "one-down." As a social species, we always notice these social differences—when others get a reward and we don't, for example.

She concluded that we have inherited brains that reward self-assertion with a good feeling (serotonin) and respond to social setbacks with a survival-threat feeling (cortisol).

The hierarchy of status is not just a human thing. Take the

---

12 You can continue learning the etymology for this word here: https://www.etymonline.com/word/status

13 Quoted from Wiktionary. https://en.wiktionary.org/wiki/status

pecking order of hens, for example. First observed and named by Norwegian zoologist and comparative psychologist Thorleif Schjelderup-Ebbe, a pecking order is a dominance hierarchy that creates an established social process among hens: one chicken always eats first and drives others away from the best part of the food, only some dare to "peck" a fight with certain others, etc.

Of course, the pecking order doesn't exist when there is only one hen, which brings us back to status as a comparison to others. Status games persist through comparison ("Keeping up with the Joneses") and exclusivity (such as "The Country Club" being shorthand for exclusive access).

The hardest truth about it is that there will always be people of a lower standing. But we actively play the game anyway, because the reward system is hardwired into our brains.

The good news is, as Paley and Elliot showed us, it doesn't have to be that way in a learning environment.

Before we move further into this subject, one thing we need to be clear about is the difference between individuals and organizations. Organizations—such as schools and the school system—have a bigger responsibility to society and the people they serve within it, as well as more social resources and policy supports. They are also the rule-makers.

Individual members of these spaces often play the status game according to the rules and rewards that the system establishes. It's possible for the participants to change the rules, and we'll talk about that in future chapters. But before that, we need to learn to see the game for what it is.

Status in the Classroom

The status game is about comparison (who is up and who is down) and exclusivity (who is in and who is out).

In the school environment, comparison plays out as competition, in both direct and indirect ways. Who is the fastest on the math test? Who is the most popular kid? Whose mom volunteers the most? Even grades are calculated by comparison and rewarded through various forms of competition.

Loretta Graziano Breuning explains in *Status Games* that every brain is just doing what it can to advance itself because that's what feels good. Often, kids don't truly understand what makes someone their friend or not. Liking someone is their main strategy. But trying to fit in to be liked can often lead to rejection of who we are—we have to abandon ourselves to fit in with others. This is not a condition where learning can happen. Persistent reminders of gaps in status accumulate into bigger negative feelings—pain, annoyance, frustration, resentment, and anger—and a more determined need to fit in and be liked.

If we agree that a focus on learning is what's needed in our schools and the school system and that our goal is to build a nurturing and supportive environment for learning to happen, then connection should be a top priority. Connection among peers is how we learn together and overcome challenges when learning gets hard.

In a learning environment, when everyone has a dream to pursue and goals to reach, peers become fellow travelers on the same journey. Measurements can focus on things like the number of projects explored or how many times they've tried again after "failing." Status can look like helping each other move forward, being kind to one another, and knowing that everyone is going to get a chance to move up. Students can be rewarded and made to feel proud for helping contribute to others' learning. This kind of peer pressure can help a learning space directed toward support and growth succeed.

But when there are no clear values and beliefs for everyone to align to, the status game runs the school's culture and eats up learning opportunities. Fears of being put down or left out not only complicate behavior but also make it easier to give up when learning gets hard.

The point of this conversation is not to get rid of status or avoid it but to figure out how to use it to help children access more learning opportunities—to build helpful markers of status. Because parental advocacy is still such an important part of the school system, when we see status-centered rewards and punishment in the classroom, a helpful question to ask would be: what can we do differently around here?

Status from Outside of the Classroom

In the Chinese public school system, parents' involvement in students' school life is largely by invitation. Teachers handle everything on the school premises, which effectively separates a student's school life from their family lives and experiences. This simplifies the learning environment in a way that has worked well for the Chinese school system.

As a parent in American schools, I had to learn how to be an involved parent—first in the public school in my neighborhood, and later in the project-based environment we moved our older son to. He and I both noticed a significant change when it came to parent involvement (recall that we are only involved at Summit when it's time to hear his presentation about his dream and personalized learning plan). Without a clear understanding of the status game and how it plays out, the more parents are involved in the classroom or class experiences, the more the status game affects school dynamics.

I remember one early volunteering experience, and a girl named Nellie, who changed my perspective completely.

Nellie was in my son's class from the start—in those early days when I was curious about the school system and how it would work for my son. Among the ways I could learn (without joining the PTA) was to chaperone certain events. I wanted to show up as much as I could, not just for my children, I told myself, but for all the children. One of the chaperone's duties was to help at a swimming class held in the nearby community center. (Swimming class was one of the nice-to-have options that not every classroom was guaranteed to experience.)

There I was, in the girl's dressing room, ready to jump in whenever kids needed me.

In the first-grade class, girls could change on their own, mostly without assistance. And since it was exciting to be in the pool, most kids moved fast. Nellie was not one who moved fast. She wasn't nearly as excited, either. While the other kids were changed or running out the door, Nellie looked around the room and then stared at a curtained changing space for a while. Other moms urged the children to go out on the deck. I mimicked their tone and said to Nellie, "Come on, girl. Hurry up! People are waiting."

Nellie turned around and asked me, "Can I use that?" pointing to the space with a curtain.

"Sure! But hurry!"

Nellie was much taller and bigger than the other girls. It was understandable that she felt conscious of her body and wanted a private space to change.

I offered to help if she needed it, but she didn't. She just wasn't in a hurry at all.

When the swimming class was over, again, most of the girls changed as fast as they could and lined up outside, ready to head back.

Nellie sat outside to catch her breath, then took her time getting dressed. I couldn't figure out what was on her mind—did she need something? She just sat there and turned to me and said something I will never forget: "I miss my mom. I wish she could be here with me."

I didn't know what to say to comfort her and asked, "Is your mom working today?" I knew that her dad had been sick for a while and her mom was busy taking care of her younger siblings.

She shook her head. "No, she isn't feeling well... I asked her to come, but she can't." She lowered her head and said in such a small voice I could barely hear:

"I miss my mom."

It struck me to the core, not only because it was from a six-year-old, but because of how she said it. That day affected me so deeply that it took a long time to see why or to know how I could talk about it.

Feelings of loneliness and sadness connected me with Nellie in a deep way. On one hand, I had this screaming loneliness inside me whenever I stepped into the school building, even when I was among all the other volunteers. From the start, I had desperately searched for acceptance from the others and tried all I could do to fit in. I wanted to be liked, hoping that one day I could finally feel at ease there. And yet, *my* presence made the kids feel uneasy.

Nellie's words were a wake-up call for me to finally see the issue that we had ignored all along: Volunteering isn't a problem. Caring for our children isn't a problem. It's when we can only see our own children and stop seeing other children that we have a problem. Especially when we're doing it to fit in. When we play the status game, we create more problems all around us. Instead of closing the status gap for schools to facilitate learning, we **enlarge** it.

Brené Brown talks about fitting in in her book *Atlas of the Heart*. This is how she defined the phrase:

Fitting in is being somewhere where you want to be, but they don't care one way or the other.

Belonging: being somewhere where you want to be, and they want you.

Fitting in is being accepted for being like everyone else.

Belonging: being accepted for being you.

Fitting in is if I have to be like you, I fit in.

Belonging: If I get to be me, I belong.

Fitting in asks us to abandon who we are.

By trying to fit in, we abandon ourselves. And when we ask children who don't feel good about the volunteer dynamics to fit in by accepting them anyway, we ask them to abandon themselves too.

Since that experience with Nellie, I made up my mind to only volunteer among adults and behind the scenes, without the presence of children. Six years later, my younger son complained to me that other parents showed up at an event while I didn't at his new elementary school. So, when the school asked parents to volunteer for a field trip a few months later, I signed up. Again, I was curious. I wanted to see if a different pedagogy and school would create a different experience for the kids.

But I drew the same conclusion—only this time, I clearly saw how much pain one particular child bore because his parents were not able to chaperone. He kept wanting to run away—not just from the children who had a parent there, but from a cruel reality that he had no power to change. When my son smiled at me and wanted to give me a hug to show how happy he was, I felt an overwhelming sense of guilt inside me and struggled to pat his back instead.

When our presence makes our own children feel great (one up) while the other children feel less (one down), are we truly helping? In what way?

To Nellie and the boy in my son's classroom, when you grow up and read this, I am sorry.

I'm sorry that I helped the system that created such pain in you and made you feel pain and loneliness. I am sorry that I believed I just needed to volunteer to fit in. I am sorry for the way the situation that I helped create affected you.

You should have a school experience where you feel that you are equal, included, accepted, and loved for who you are, no matter what resources or capacity your family has.

Status in the Learning Environment

In the Creatives Workshop at Akimbo, our status is marked by our contributions to others. Since the workshop was built on the value of generosity, we are encouraged to contribute to other people's learning journeys by giving feedback, comments, and suggestions. Peers also support each other through group settings to create further intimacy and deeper connection. The more a person supports the others, the more this person is considered a leader by the others. Leading in the workshop won't get us fancy titles and there is no monetary reward, only people's respect and trust. Leading is serving, and it's a choice we make.

Creativity is another way that people assign our status. We see each other through the lens of our active creation and practice. Instead of comparing our creativity to someone else's, we are interested in each other's ultimate success with their projects and the destinations we are all heading toward.

Meanwhile, my older son pointed out the drastic differences between Summit Public Schools and his previous neighborhood school. He said that he didn't see the same kind of status games at Summit that he experienced in our neighborhood school: favoritism because of students' families, popularity contests among children, and the ultimate privilege that came with each. The key is that Summit is aware of the status game and specifically created the school around what is required for learning to happen.

When schools and learning spaces create new status norms, with the intention of supporting everyone as they learn, the community that forms within the school can change how students interact with learning and one another.

Chapter 8:
The Power Hierarchy

I didn't know about Dr. Seuss until we had our first child. The first book we got was *Dr. Seuss's ABC*, and we all loved it enormously. But for all the time spent reading to them and gathering stories they would love, I wasn't introduced to *Yertle the Turtle* until 2020, when Seth Godin linked to it inside of a blog post.[14]

Many of Dr. Suess's stories have profound meanings even for adults to absorb—*How the Grinch Stole Christmas*, *The Lorax*, *Oh the Places You'll Go*. But I found the level of cruelty depicted in *Yertle the Turtle* to be off-the-charts accurate. Especially when it comes to top-down management cultures.

The story of Yertle is about the turtle king of a pond on the imagined island of Sala-ma-Sond. All the turtles were happy, enjoying their pond and all the provisions within it. Then Yertle decided that it wasn't enough to just rule the turtles in their happy little pond. He wanted more.

The answer, he decided, was to make his throne tall enough to see beyond the pond, and if he could see more then he could rule more. And that throne, he declared, would be lifted higher by resting it on the backs of other turtles.

One by one, he added more and more turtles to his throne, until he could see all around.

Yertle was quite pleased with himself ("Oh, marvelous me! For I am the ruler of all that I see!"), despite the complaints from a turtle at the very bottom of the stack. There, a "plain little turtle" named Mack quietly informed Yertle of how difficult it was to hold the entire stack, throne, and king on his back.

---

14 For this post, and to follow the rest of his blog, go here: https://seths. blog/2020/11/the-persistence-of-hierarchy-and-status-roles/

Instead of compassion, Yertle only felt more pride. He commanded more turtles to join the stack, threatening them until: "They trembled. They shook. But they came. They obeyed."

Mack kept speaking up, and Yertle kept stacking turtles up, now convinced that he had to be taller than the moon if he was to be truly great.

Finally, while Yertle is marveling at how tall his turtle stack had made him, from the very bottom of the stack, Mack does something simple that proves to be revolutionary: he burps.

His burp shakes the throne so much that Yertle is plunked right back into the pond, to become King of the Mud, which is "all he can see," while the other turtles are released to be free as "all creatures should be."

When I read this book to my children, they both expressed their clear dislike for Yertle, even though they couldn't yet grasp concepts of hierarchy and oppression. The characters' actions and impact were enough to give them their impressions: "Yertle is a bad turtle," and "Poor Mack, he is hungry."

When we asked what they liked about the story, they both said, "Burp!"

I, too, felt a sense of relief every time we made it to the end. Mack was OK. He got to protect his shell and end his and the others' suffering in the most natural way possible. The turtles got to be themselves again. Dr. Seuss turned the mountain of hierarchy and oppression into a molehill of the turtle tower.

Taking a cue from Dr. Seuss, we will not discuss whether the hierarchy is good or bad in this chapter. Just like everything else, it exists for a reason and will continue to exist. But we will look at the actions and impacts of hierarchy in the school environment to see if it actually helps kids learn or study, or if someone, somewhere, is about to burp.

Hierarchy and Leadership

When Seth Godin created the Akimbo Workshops in 2015, he set out to teach people a new way to see the world. The primary value that guides the operations in Akimbo and everyone within it, including students, is generosity. Akimbo believes giving helps more than taking, and that the forward motion of generosity brings people together to tackle individual challenges more sustainably. As students, we found this to be true. The more we give to and share with others, the faster we learn and the more we are willing to receive from others.

This redefined our sense of status so that service was rewarded more than performance, which shifted the dynamics of leadership as well. The structure of the Akimbo Workshops—pre-recorded lectures with live coaching when necessary—maximized each student's autonomy, acceptance for both self and others, and peer-to-peer support meeting learning needs. We were encouraged to solve problems in an interdependent way, which you don't experience in other learning spaces or institutions. The transactional and reciprocal model (I do this for you so that you will do something back for me) is much more common, making generous peer-to-peer support and positive peer pressure (I support you so that you can help others, while others support more people, and the whole ecosystem becomes better – pay it forward) the kind of change that shows us how the world can be.

This horizontal structure reminds me of what Malcolm Gladwell wrote in *The Tipping Point,* using Gore Associates as an example: "Gore doesn't need formal management structure in its small plants (150 people)—it doesn't need the usual layer of middle and upper management—because in groups that small, informal personal relationships are more effective. A longtime associate in the company said, 'This is what you get when you have small teams, where everybody knows everybody. Peer pressure is much more powerful than the concept of a boss.

Many, many times more powerful. People want to live up to what is expected of them.'"

No hierarchy is needed in Akimbo because every person in the community depends on others to learn, connect, and thrive. Job titles are simply ways to differentiate various roles. And status is about generosity rather than competition and winning.

Seth believes in individual and collective learning through trial and error, care, and empathy toward the people we seek to serve. If I can't practice my learning and feedback skills with peers, I will certainly have a much harder time with others I expect to lead or collaborate with.

Now, just like the goal is not to avoid or get rid of status but to create a healthy reward system that everyone can pursue, the school doesn't have to eliminate leadership roles either. Remember, before Yertle's desire to rule "the cat, the cow, and the house," he was already the king of a nice little pond. "It was clean. It was neat. The water was warm. There was plenty to eat. The turtles had everything a turtle might need." And all the turtles were "quite happy indeed." Having a turtle king wasn't a problem. Yertle was the king and the others enjoyed their lives too. The problem was when Yertle stopped supporting everyone's well-being in the pond on the island of Sala-ma-Sond and only cared about making his throne higher. When reaching the moon became more important than the life or death of the turtles beneath him, Yertle himself became the problem.

Leadership is a form of service, and in the instance of school, the students are the ones being served. If that's ever *not* the case, the whole system is upside down.

This can be hard to see, however, because of how often "leading" is used to mean "managing," and managing to mean power. And in those scenarios, both leading and managing are ways to gain status rather than to serve. Healthy leadership is a key part of this transformation.

If positions and tactics of leadership are used to help everyone—including every child, every family, and each school employee, then it is true leadership guiding the community toward students' and families' goals.

If leading means the system ensures the system's "needs" are met and sustained, then the school leadership team isn't leading at all—they are managing and responding to the system. And that has little to do with the needs of children who can't speak up for themselves and families fighting for ways to speak up and be heard.

Yertle had a goal that nobody else but him cared about, and when Mack's feedback didn't align with this goal, Mack became a "problem". In this Yertle-centered culture, ignoring Mack and letting things get worse for him made sense. We are not turtles, and we can certainly do better than Yertle. But we do need to focus on optimizing our children's learning opportunities and overall well-being rather than prioritizing their participation in arbitrary reward systems and compliance with authority figures at all costs. If we're not careful to prioritize learning, we could be following each other into a system-centered turtle stack without realizing it.

What the BLT Taught Me About Hierarchy

In all the Building Leadership Team meetings I attended, the main focus always revolved around the priority goals within the Continuous School Improvement Plan—how to work within the budget for the next school year and staff arrangements that would accomplish those goals from within our many constraints.

There was little room for teachers and staff members to submit their own discussion topics and even fewer opportunities for parents to raise a concern or propose an idea. For each BLT meeting, according to the bylaws, every member has the opportunity to propose an agenda item for the team to discuss. At first, I thought we could propose any concerns that we had if it was relevant to our children and school. However, it turned out that only what was directly related to the continuous development plan was supported.

The school was open to hearing what parents had to say when we got the opportunity, but there was no real discussion or solution-finding beyond that. Over and over, I got the same message: *Yes, we hear you. But this is the way our system runs.* If our problems happened to be the same problems, they would get addressed. But when that was not the case, tough luck! Once again, it became clear that running the system had very little to do with the parents' satisfaction.

The principal had the most access to information, so without his presence, we couldn't make any decisions. One time, when the principal had to attend another event and the BLT meeting carried on without him, staff and teachers tried to make decisions anyway but simply didn't have enough information to do so. After an hour and a half, the meeting adjourned with nothing accomplished.

The divisions of power and status were obvious. Not only were parents not fully given a voice important enough to influence change, but some team members were clearly on the opposite side of the principal as well. Years later, I learned that it was likely because they were part of opposing groups. The teachers' union, for example, is separate from the principal's administration backing. When the two top-down worldviews are not aligned with each other but are forced to "lead" within the same school, it results in constant power struggles with escalating conflicts.

This would rarely happen in other organizations or even independent schools. Most of the time, once a clear purpose and goals are articulated by the leadership team, employees can decide whether they align with them or not. When discovering the misalignment, people often choose to quit and find a different organization with whom they align. Not a problem at all. There is no need to force two different value systems or worldviews to work together, believing things will work out on their own (they often don't). Especially in today's social and political environment, most of us have very little tolerance for differences as important as values and beliefs. But this was what happened in our school. When the value and belief gap is more significant than the possibilities of working together, and being relocated from one school to another impacts the principal or teacher's career too much, people fall into conflicts instead of making a choice.

The school system needs to run on what's working for the system. What our children need is a separate issue. When the two overlap, things work for everyone. When they do not, families leave.

People assumed it was safe for the parent representative to stay neutral, and it was—until neutrality wasn't safe anymore. The principal was supported by the public school system. Teachers and staff members were supported by their unions. But parent representatives were on our own, regardless of whether we had the PTA in our corner.

In the BLT, I proposed we start team meetings with personal sharing on two approved questions, hoping this would change the atmosphere from a value clash to the potential for connection. My proposal was approved, but only some felt safe enough to open up and share. Tension was constantly high, and that disconnect had a ripple effect throughout the school.

Losing the art program was a great example: students and parents voted to keep art as well as music. The BLT voted to let the art program go, with two reasons to support this decision: the art teacher relinquished the position to honor the music teacher's higher seniority and full-time position because hiring a new art teacher and a new music teacher would be too much for our school to handle. Letting the art program go satisfied everyone's needs and desires—except for our children's.

As parents, we know when something isn't right. For a long time, I tried to dismiss the persistent feeling of not belonging in school. Then I tried to volunteer to find some peace of mind. When that failed, I tried to donate money to feel like I was part of the school. I tried to join the PTA and ended up in the BLT. All the way, I tried to talk myself out of the gut-wrenching feelings I had about many things, but nothing worked.

The fear and tension that came with my role in the BLT were off the charts. No parents would disagree with the team members without worrying about the possibility of backlash directed toward their children. I was no exception. When important issues are not discussed by the leadership team, where else are we to talk about them? How else are we to solve them?

Instead of staying frustrated and upset, I started to become curious. How did this system *really* work, and why?

Chapter 9:
What Is School For?

It's nearly impossible to talk about the system without getting to the root of it all—the purpose of school itself. When I started to ask my podcast guests "What is school for?" they had all kinds of answers. That's when I took a step back and realized that we don't even have a shared understanding of what school is for, much less how to improve it. Here are some of the answers I heard:

- *"A school is for providing students with the tools which become keys to open whatever doors they want to open in their future... A school is or should be for providing students with the confidence to find out their passion, gifts, and dreams."* —Neveen M.

- *"School is for creating opportunity... for yourself or for the student, to be that critical thinker, that problem solver, that creative individual... our job in public schools is to create learners who ask the right questions."* —Anette C.

- *"I believe that school is for developing and meeting the academic, social, psychological, emotional, and physical needs of children, whatever they are on any given day."* —John B.

- *"I think it's for social and emotional development, academic development, and more emphasis on work ethic and striving for excellence."* —Weili G.

- *"I think the goal is very broad. It is just to raise future well-trained, well-equipped citizens of the country."* —Ingrid G.

In chapter four, we talked about the documentary *Waiting for "Superman,"* where director Davis Guggenheim talked about the purpose of our modern public school system. He included this about the expectations of the school system:

*"Schools like Woodside are doing the job they were designed for fifty years ago. The system of tracking fits the demands of the time. Only **20 percent** of high school graduates are expected to go to college. They will become doctors, lawyers, and CEOs. The **next 20 percent** are meant to go straight into skilled jobs like accountants, managers, and bureaucrats. And the **bottom 60 percent** become workers like farmers and factory workers. There were jobs for everyone in the booming post-war economy, and schools like Woodside did their part to supply a useful workforce. The problem is, our schools haven't changed but the world around them has."*

Our schools haven't changed, but the world around them has.

The ultimate purpose of our public school system—and the reason for its top-down hierarchical culture—has been to support the employment needs of our society and economy, not to help our children thrive. And it isn't even doing that well.

There are many things worth talking about here. First, the hypothesis this system started from was that "getting a job" was all schools needed to prepare kids for. That's how standardized tests came to measure what they do and why schools send students on different tracks based on their most likely career paths. As a result, the school system has played an active role in limiting kids to the tiers of society the school believes they belong within.

Ultimately, this entire approach is based on a scarcity mentality that says only a few can truly succeed, and if you can't reach the top, you are destined to be at the bottom. Schools are designed to find the children who might make it to the top and funnel the rest into ordinary, mass majority lives. This kind of belief drives many parents' fears that their children have to be the best or are simply not good students at all. However, the world has changed since the start of the public school system and continues to change from generation to generation.

While we still worry about whether our children will do well in life, I don't know how many parents send their children to school so they can get a factory or farm job after they graduate. I don't even know how many parents would agree that any job is the reason their kids go to school. Especially after the pandemic shifted all our perceptions of the world, we know that success means something different for each individual.

As a society, we have progressed enough to know that it is not about what kind of job we do, but how we do it—as Seth Godin writes in *The Song of Significance*, "washing a car is significant if you do it right." There, he tells a lovely story about Rising Tide Car Wash and how they have changed people's lives through their business—employees and customers alike. Their four guiding principles demonstrate the kind of environment that people need to thrive: a feeling of safety, a culture of accountability, a clear purpose, and customer love.

If a car wash can demonstrate a better way of life, it's clear that being significant has nothing to do with income level, public perception, or social status. It's about choosing to make a difference. This is undoubtedly why people are leaving their "successful" careers as doctors, lawyers, and CEOs and the amount of stress that they endured with them. Change allows them a second chance at life, to truly explore, learn what they are interested in and passionate about, and pursue their dreams instead of inherited definitions of success from family or society. Working for money and status alone, without enjoying what you do, isn't a sustainable way of living, and the kind of work we get to choose to do today was unimaginable at the time when the public school system was created.

Technology and the Internet have changed the way we work, learn, study, live, and connect with one another. The world has opened over time, not closed, with more opportunities to connect with information and one another than ever before. As a result, our dream jobs aren't defined by an impersonal system, but by our own knowing and guidance. Everyone has an opportunity and the capacity to discover and fulfill their highest potential, and learning and studying should be the first to offer that to us.

The question of what school is for, then, really comes down to this: are school and work the means to an end or the end itself? If getting a job is all there is to life, they are an end. But if school and work are necessary components of a *fulfilled life*, they are a means.

I believe schools and jobs are a means to an end in life.

I believe that schools are important places to help our children learn about themselves—their own passions, interests, and dreams—and about each other and the world. I believe that their learning and studying are meant to prepare them to do what they love when they grow up, to lead a fulfilled life, and to be contributing members of society.

Most importantly, I believe school can be a place to nurture and support kids, to create the conditions for them to learn about their own knowing and self-trust, and a first place to experience true belonging.

The Search for Belonging

When our family went to our very first open house event at the neighborhood school, I had a clear feeling that we were outsiders who didn't belong.

When I attended my first PTA meeting after a year of being in the school, I was still an outsider.

In my last year at the Building Leadership Team, I finally had friendships and connections with some parents and team members, yet the feeling of exclusion persisted.

I couldn't wrap my head around this. On the surface, everything sounded welcoming and inviting, but reality felt very different.

Deep down, I knew something wasn't right. But instead of questioning what I saw and experienced, I chose to question myself. I criticized myself for being sensitive and overthinking.

In her book, *Song of Increase*, Jacqueline Freeman said that "knowing exists before we learn to think." She compared this knowing to the way bees learn how to restore their well-being and hive—a deeply instinctual feeling. In *Untamed,* Glennon Doyle called knowing "warm liquid gold." Knowing is the most earnest inquiry we send to ourselves and the deepest truth that responds from within. Knowing doesn't require status or money, but it can be buried under the distractions of each, hiding behind the noise of our busy lives. It offers an answer that may not exist on the internet, in books, or in the external world at all.

When things don't add up, when we know that there is something wrong, missing, or buried, that is the beginning of knowing.

Unfortunately, we often stop seeking what we need to know in those moments, usually because we are afraid of what we'll find. The unknown may lead to inconvenient truths—about the system, the culture, the hierarchy, the rewards and punishments, and the beliefs behind all of them. That can be frightening, but *not* knowing is just one part of our fear. How it might resolve, especially when we are not certain that there is any resolution, is the truly terrifying part of the unknown.

This is where I stayed for a while: *Maybe what I'm feeling isn't normal. Maybe it's better that I just bury my head in the sand, pretending that everything is OK. Maybe the discomfort will eventually go away. Maybe it is safest to swallow "the burp."*

But every time I learned something was not working for my children, I started to feel this hopeless guilt and concern all over again.

The Search for Safety

When there were conflicts in BLT meetings, fear and tension ran high. No one wanted to make a mistake that might lead to unwanted consequences, especially if those affected their children. In a top-down system with low transparency, speculation piques more curiosity and sends some parents running, looking even harder to find safety and clarity.

It's important to notice that there is a difference between tension and fear. Creatives, for example, use tension to their advantage by creating works that matter, solving problems, making commitments, and putting ourselves on the hook to make a difference. Fear is also an effective tool, but it's used within hierarchies to build authority and reward compliance. But fear doesn't actually help anyone, and it is especially damaging if we want to learn, create, connect, and do better by challenging our limits. When fear is running through our schools, classrooms, and meetings, we feel small, lonely, powerless, and scared. And in an environment with an obvious power hierarchy, we often feel and see fear everywhere.

As humans, we tame fear by seeking the seemingly safe shelter and security of connection—with other parents, sometimes even teachers and staff members. But in this situation, where there is no real community and everyone is busy fending for themselves, who do you stand with? To feel safe, we need to feel like we belong. And to do that in such a divided environment, we almost always need to abandon ourselves.

After I experienced real welcome and a truly inviting, safe environment in the Akimbo Workshops, I no longer wondered whether it was just my imagination that I didn't belong in the PTA or school. It was clear that, regardless of the words that were used to communicate "welcoming" or "in partnership," words alone wouldn't welcome all parents into the space.

This is a constant challenge in the school system: reality often contradicts the messages we are given. The gap between the reality that we are the customers of the public schools and the feeling that we are helpless within them was the most common frustration I heard from parents that I interviewed, communicated with, and connected with in various groups. When that gap is big enough, it not only costs trust but eventually our choice with the system altogether.

As it turns out, there is a word to describe these mismatches: *performance*.

Brené Brown wrote about cultivating meaningful connection in *Atlas of the Heart*, describing the way something that appears to be a connection can turn out to be disconnection. She calls this subtle but driving force the "near enemy," and more obvious disconnection as the "far enemy." When we haven't learned the differences, we mistake "near enemy" as a connection. Since it isn't the same as obvious disconnection, it is merely a performance.

According to her, "On the surface, the near enemies of emotions or experiences might look and even feel like connection, but ultimately they drive us to be disconnected from ourselves and from each other. Without awareness, near enemies become practices that fuel separation, rather than practices that reinforce the inextricable connection of all people."

To name some examples: A group claims a non-judgmental practice, but people experience judgment everywhere. A physician claims she cares about you, but when you express your concerns about potential medical bills, she immediately tells you how much *she* had to pay for *her* bills and that your cost was nothing compared to hers. Or the popular 'show-and-tell' day in school, where every child in the class can bring a toy and talk about it, and the kids end up focusing on how cool their toys look compared to the others.

I imagine the original show-and-tell activity was designed to help children with observation, self-expression, and sharing something they love. A show-and-tell with a student's creation or experience with a book they love would foster interest, love, and enthusiasm. Children would have the chance to learn more about one another, share their excitement, and celebrate accomplishments.

When a system is intentionally designed to create hierarchical outcomes—we support some students and expect them to do well, but not so much the rest—it turns into a system that only works for the top 20 or 40 percent of kids.

These performances may not be intentional on all levels of the system, but the clear underlying belief is that not everyone can study well—that not everyone can succeed in schools.

If we want to agree on who and what schools are for, and what values, beliefs, and worldviews shape that opinion, we must look into the culture, not the strategy.

Chapter 10:
The Invisible Hand of Culture

"Culture eats strategy for breakfast."
—Anonymous

Writing this book has been a journey beyond what I imagined it would be. What started as an attempt to make sense of a confusing, difficult time in the school system turned into a bigger question about school itself and the culture that shapes it.

My lived experience as both a student and a parent showed me that learning and studying are two different things. They are both simply activities, but the way they are organized in different environments can create different outcomes. Stepping into this book, I knew that culture played a crucial role in the environment, but I didn't have a larger understanding of what that actually meant and how it would affect the outcome of learning and studying.

Understanding culture helps us see why things happen the way they do.

When parents have feedback and requests, we expect to hear answers and responses from the system because we believe that we are the customers and that listening to customers' feedback is how the school system improves its services. But then we find out that's rarely how things go within the school system.

It isn't because the system hasn't heard us, but because the system was set up for something else.

And, it turns out, culture is a big topic that can be a book on its own. What we need for *this* book is a cultural framework that helps us understand our school system in relationship to its purpose, the parties involved, and the opportunities that are presented to us. Because if we aren't seeing the system through the lens of culture, we aren't seeing it in its entirety.

Understanding Organizational Culture Styles

When seeking the answer to the question "What is school for?", the more I compared Summit Public Schools and our neighborhood schools, the more questions I had about organizational culture. In my search for answers, I came across a 2018 study published by Boris Groysberg, et al., in *Harvard Business Review*. It was titled "The Culture Factor," and it covered 230 companies and 1,300 executives across a range of industries and regions, from public to private to nonprofit, along with survey responses from 25,000 employees and company managers about their experience of work.

The goal was to identify the impact of culture, beginning with the nature of culture: *shared* among people in the group or community; *pervasive and enduring,* permeating multiple levels and applying deeply and broadly in an organization (deeply trenched) over a long period; and *implicit*—a silent language that people recognize and respond to instinctively.

Ultimately, they determined what parents already feel in public schools, as I experienced and as *Waiting for "Superman"* demonstrated: Until we can change a system's culture and purpose (our collective goal), changing strategies is a non-productive waste of resources and time.

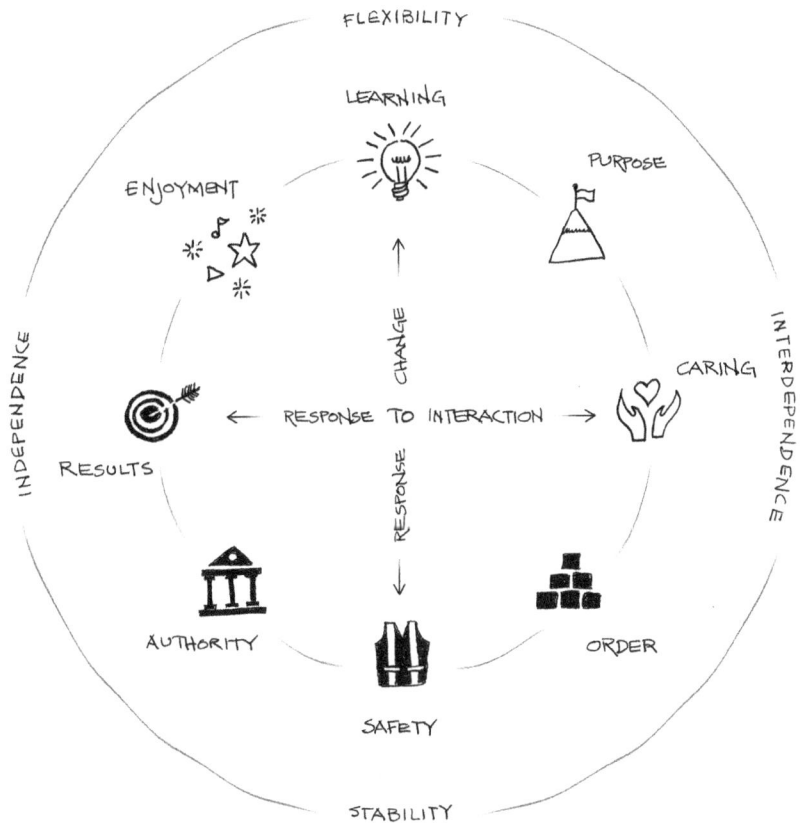

Eight Organizational Culture Styles

This illustration is inspired by Spencer Stuart's Culture Alignment Framework illustration:
https://www.spencerstuart.com/what-we-do/our-capabilities/leadership-consulting/
organizational-culture

Before we go further, here are a few things we should keep in mind when learning about organizational cultural styles:

- *There are NO good or bad cultural styles. Every style has pros and cons and exists to serve a purpose.*

* *A helpful lens to place on different styles is whether it serves the organization's purpose and goals.*

- *Even though culture is largely strategized and defined by the leadership team and executive level, everyone has the power to contribute to and influence the change of culture.*

According to the Culture Factor report, there are a total of eight culture styles: authority, order, safety, learning, enjoyment, purpose, caring, and results. They went on to explain the pros and cons of each, as well as the connections between culture and the outcomes, staff engagement and motivation, and customer relationships.

Notice the axis dividing this chart, as they are important identifications. These represent the common threads that they identified as what distinguishes one culture style from another: how human interactions play out and how resilient the organization is to change.

The first axis indicates the level of resilience toward change, ranging from the most flexible to the least, separating the top half of the map from the bottom half. The second axis indicates the level of interaction and engagement among people, ranging from interdependence (the collective) to independence (the individual). This divides the right half from the left half.

Given those divisions, the following four are *flexible* and *change-resilient* styles, taken from the Culture Factor report:

Caring *focuses on relationships and mutual trust. Caring environments are warm, collaborative, and welcoming places where people help and support one another. Employees are united by loyalty; leaders emphasize sincerity, teamwork, and positive relationships.*

> ***Advantages:*** *Improved teamwork, engagement, communication, trust, and sense of belonging.*

> ***Disadvantages:*** *Overemphasis on consensus building may reduce exploration of options, stifle competitiveness, and slow decision-making.*

Purpose *is exemplified by idealism and altruism. Purpose-driven environments are tolerant, compassionate places where people try to do good for the long-term future of the world. Employees are united by a focus on sustainability and global communities; leaders emphasize shared ideas and contributions to a greater cause.*

> ***Advantages:*** *Improved appreciation for diversity, sustainability, and social responsibility.*

> ***Disadvantages:*** *Overemphasis on a long-term purpose and ideals may get in the way of practical and immediate concerns.*

Learning *is characterized by exploration, expansiveness, and creativity. Learning environments are inventive and open-minded places that spark new ideas and encourage people to explore alternatives. Employees are united by curiosity; leaders emphasize innovation, knowledge, and adventure.*

> ***Advantages:*** *Improved innovation, agility, and organizational learning.*

Disadvantages: *Overemphasis on exploration may lead to a lack of focus and an inability to exploit existing disadvantages.*

Enjoyment *is expressed through fun and excitement. Enjoyment-focused environments are lighthearted places where people tend to do what makes them happy. Employees are united by playfulness and stimulation, while leaders emphasize spontaneity and a sense of humor.*

Advantages: *Improved employee morale, engagement, and creativity.*

Disadvantages: *Overemphasis on autonomy and engagement may lead to a lack of discipline and create possible compliance or governance issues.*

And these four are *stability-focused* and *change-resistant* styles, again quoted:

Order *is focused on respect, structure, and shared norms. These environments are methodical places where people tend to play by the rules and want to fit in. Employees in an order culture are united by cooperation; leaders emphasize shared procedures and time-honored customs.*

Advantages: *Improved operational efficiency, reduced conflict, and greater civic-mindedness.*

Disadvantages: *Overemphasis on rules and traditions may reduce individuation, stifle creativity, and limit organizational agility.*

Safety *is defined by planning, caution, and preparedness. Work environments are predictable places where people are risk-conscious and think things through carefully. Employees are united by a desire to feel protected and to anticipate change, and leaders emphasize being realistic and planning ahead.*

Advantages: Improved risk management, stability, and business continuity.

Disadvantages: Overemphasis on standardization and formalization may lead to bureaucracy, inflexibility, and dehumanization of the work environment.

Authority *is defined by strength, decisiveness, and boldness. Authoritative work environments are competitive places where individuals strive to gain a personal advantage. Employees are united by a strong sense of control, while leaders emphasize confidence and dominance.*

Advantages: Improved speed of decision-making and responsiveness to threats or crises.

Disadvantages: Overemphasis on strong authority and bold decision-making may lead to politics, conflict, and a psychologically unsafe work environment.

Results *cultures are characterized by achievement and winning. These environments are outcome-oriented, merit-based places where people aspire to achieve top performance. Employees are united by a drive for capability and success; leaders emphasize goal accomplishment.*

Advantages: Improved execution, external focus, capability building, and goal achievement.

Disadvantages: Overemphasis on achieving results may lead to communication and collaboration breakdowns and higher levels of stress and anxiety.

The study also noted that "culture is a more elusive lever" when compared to strategies, "because much of it is anchored in unspoken behaviors, mindsets, and social patterns." Yet even though it is elusive, culture is still the most effective lever we have for real change.

The Two Camps

According to the Culture Factor research, results and caring are universal culture styles across organization types, sizes, regions, and industries. They appeared in every organization and system across the board and represent two ends of the scale of human interaction: Results-dominant cultures emphasize achievement and independence, while Caring-dominant cultures focus on the collective's well-being and goals. Most organizations fall somewhere in between, balancing desired outcomes from both teamwork and individual results, which puts the axis between **Results** and **Caring**.

Looking at the chart's **top half** and **bottom half** is a helpful way to see a culture in one of two camps: either resilient toward change or resistant toward change. The top half embraces change, engagement, and motivation, and are customer-oriented culture styles. The cultures in the bottom half focus on maintaining the status quo and applying standardization for stability—system-oriented culture styles.

Remember, there is no bad culture style on this map. What matters is the connection between culture and the organization's defined purpose and goals.

Purpose, Learning, and Enjoyment are customer-oriented cultures where empathy, connection, learning, and engagement are maximized to adapt to changes and innovate. With Learning culture in the middle, we see the balance between Caring and Results cultures creating a maximized outcome. The main characteristics of these cultures include caring about and listening to customers' feedback, criticism, and requests to explore and make changes accordingly.

The cultural styles on the opposite side serve a very different purpose. **Authority, Safety, and Order** are system-oriented cultures, where operational efficiency, risk management, continuity, and crisis management are enhanced and executed to meet stability goals. Among these culture styles, following rules, applying standards, and upholding a strong sense of authority are the main attributes. These culture styles aren't centered around customers, they serve the system or subsystem instead.

With this understanding, let's take a closer look at our public school system.

Systems and Subsystems

Different systems and subsystems run on different cultures. These can be easy to spot in some organizations, especially when they are smaller or have a simple structure. But a school system is neither small nor simple. It includes *the school administration* (which runs the school district and employs the superintendent and school principals), *the teachers union*, the *Parent Teacher Association* (the PTA), and local schools—(including neighborhood schools and option schools). Each of these entities has its own culture combination style.

The Administration: Authority and Safety

The school administration rarely changes the way the system operates. It's not because the administration hasn't heard us but because they have chosen to operate without our input. The purpose of the system has determined that they are not bent on what students and parents need but focus exclusively on what it was set up to do. The loss of the art program is just one example of many. The Authority culture is in place to support and sustain what the school needs as the top focus and priority. The two measurements that my school district provided are clear examples of standardization: the percentage pass rates and the "safe and welcoming environment" standards.

It's a common practice for students to be prepared for tests months ahead, likely because the pass rate for the school is connected directly with some level of their funding, sometimes even determining its survival. Using attendance as the measurement for a safe and welcoming environment instead of conditioning for connection, peer support, and acceptance misses important areas such as emotional and psychological safety.

Seeing the Authority and Safety cultures helps us to pay attention to the decisions they are making and understand what we are seeing through these cultural lenses.

The Teachers Union: Order and Safety

When the art teacher walked away from our neighborhood school, the decision gained applause from her fellow teachers. She respected the music teacher as her senior and honored that long-lasting tradition despite the results of our survey. She cared about her work, her peers, and her students tremendously and did a remarkable job teaching. What I learned from her departure is the power of an Order culture.

The dominant cultures among teachers appear to be Order and Safety. Recall that Order is united by cooperation and that leaders emphasize shared procedures and time-honored customs. This explains the importance of lining up by seniority, which ultimately decided the fate of our art program. In the Safety culture, employees are united by a desire to feel protected and to anticipate change, which explains the emphasis on tenure. Teachers with tenure will not be dismissed from their jobs for almost any reason, but instead are moved to the same job in a different school. The documentary *Waiting for "Superman"* demonstrates the Safety culture of the union, loud and clear.

Overemphasizing seniority, adhering to tradition, and following rules are the main behaviors in Order culture. Combined with Safety, it strengthens teamwork, protection, and cooperation among teachers, but with consequences. This form of standardization can lead to dehumanization in a work environment by denying individuation (the uniqueness of human beings) and limiting creativity.

There is a difference between Order culture and structure in school. In previous chapters, Akimbo and Summit Public Schools demonstrated the purpose of structure. But Order culture is about fitting in according to a status rank. When status is not addressed and mitigated, the Order culture fosters and nurtures favoritism, preferential treatment, and a rewards system that encourages abandonment of self as a whole. Organizational structure alone doesn't necessarily create or support these challenges. Both Akimbo and Summit Public Schools have structure, but the dominant culture is Learning.

The PTA System: Order

An Order culture led our neighborhood school's parent volunteers to believe that a parent-based art program was a great option, even though parents were aware there was no comparison between that and a formal school curriculum. An amateur program may have met some parents' need to contribute and play along in the status game, but it would have lowered the average quality of the art program for the children. And what's even more damaging, it sent a wrong signal to students that the subject they connected to wasn't worth speaking up for.

In an Order culture, harmony and peace are overemphasized, to fit in and comply instead of advocating for improvements and change. When we stop advocating for what our children need and simply volunteer to fit in, we are taking the shortcut in a race to the bottom without even realizing it.

There is nothing wrong with wanting to help out, but civic-mindedness should not stop us from holding the system and schools accountable for providing quality learning opportunities. If the PTA is only organizing parents in volunteering, not advocacy, they have moved away from the change that the two founders set out to make "when women did not have the right to vote, and social activism was not popular. However, they believed mothers would support their mission to eliminate threats that endangered children, and in early 1897, they started a nationwide campaign."

If Alice McLellan Birney and Phoebe Apperson Hearst simply followed what was established in the society and were busy running around to volunteer and play status games, they would've said nothing and complied instead of speaking up and putting their collective foot down to support children.

Since it was founded in 1897, the PTA has done some tremendous work advocating for children. But for decades, PTA member enrollment has been declining nationwide, and in my last year with the BLT at our neighborhood school, only about 10 percent of parents in our school were PTA members. Besides membership decline, "effective contribution from parents" today means something very different than in 1897.

Like the public school system, the PTA hasn't changed. But the world around it has.

When parent involvement has become a predictable source of status games and power struggles that further enhance popularity and favoritism, we help to create the divide in school. Our very presence furthers the inequity gaps that we set out to close. As stated in chapter seven, there is nothing wrong with working toward a status, but it's our responsibility to build status that helps students and our schools instead of causing more problems.

Instead of defaulting to an Order culture, we can choose the culture we create to learn about our children and each other.

Local Schools: Order, Safety, and Authority

Each local school is a subsystem of its own. This is the place where children and families meet the principal, teachers, and staff members. Both Caring and Results cultures should be equally important here, as building trust and emphasizing outcomes are two strong reasons why families are willing to give schools the benefit of the doubt and join in the first place.

Unfortunately, instead of a customer-focused culture such as Learning, Purpose, and Enjoyment, the dominant culture combination at our neighborhood school is Authority, Order, and Safety. This is the combination of the administration, the teachers union, and the PTA. Instead of having a separate school culture, we have pass-through styles from all the subsystems in the greater school system umbrella.

In the first chapters of this book, we saw that studying is the typical experience of school, where the goal of passing standardized tests drives all the decisions and guides everything done around the school. Tests are one-time events that define success and failure (not just for students, but also for teachers, the principal, and the school), building toward the priority goal that indicates and directs the school's focus.

Besides grades and test results, winning—in sports, competitions, and even being popular or succeeding at the status games—is another common occurrence in our schools. This recognition is typically credited back to an individual rather than the collective. Where we could build peer support and raise expectations for one another, getting ahead as an individual is more commonly praised.

When it comes to learning as we define it—abundant choices to enroll in and no grading in place by any means—there are rarely any learning opportunities at our neighborhood school. The afterschool enrichment is the closest to real learning kids get, but even that is inaccessible for many students who depend on the school bus service. For students who were able to attend, the cost was not accessible to everyone. And, since COVID, the afterschool enrichment program has stopped entirely. Some parents might ask whether music and art are learning opportunities. Again, when students don't have abundant choices that reflect their diverse human intelligence (the very reason that parents fought for art) and when students' performances are recorded on report cards, these subjects have become about studying. Besides that, since they are not the priority goal for schools, they are eliminated first whenever the school faces budget cuts or low projections for the next school year.

What's missing in studying-focused schools isn't experience or time, but opportunities to dream and the structure in place to support those dreams throughout the school years. There isn't a well-designed structure in place supporting students to dream about life beyond jobs, because schools were designed to supply a workforce. Even then, students are underprepared for college and hesitate about choosing a major. Many students and families pay expensive tuition only to find out they are interested in something else. Remember Henry's story? He's not alone. These are cultural differences.

Culture gets complicated in local schools.

Almost every conflict we have seen in local schools is cultural. This is not because students and families do not understand or don't value our schools but because the world has changed while the schools haven't. The internet alone has given us abundant choices and connections that enable us to learn and create. Everywhere we go, we have options that support our individual needs, well-being, and life goals instead of fitting into a place where we are constantly rejected or have to abandon ourselves to fit in.

When the BLT chose music over art, it met many needs: the needs of the teachers and staff members, the needs of the school administration, and the needs for operations. But it also left unmet needs in students and families, as well as some teachers and staff members who weren't sure about the solution or were wondering why things had to be this way.

Whenever the BLT needed to finalize a budget proposal within two or three days, it would happen despite team members asking for more days to process and gather feedback and consensus. The most space we got was a one or two-day extension as an exception. It was frustrating in many ways, but it met the system's need for efficiency. Because conflicts in schools are cultural conflicts with beliefs and values that run deeper in each group, the limited timeframe intensified disagreements and power struggles, which led to a divided and fearful environment. The vibe eventually trickled down to students and families.

Over the increasing demands to be heard, seen, and understood by parents, we were advocating for the change of culture—from system-centered to customer-oriented—while schools have been operating from a culture of stability all along.

Different from the school system and the other subsystems, in schools, students and families are important participants in the engagement loop. Negative events do have consequences, particularly among families who have the buying power to decide what to do with their school choice. When facing pressure around physical and emotional safety and feeling the scarcity of public school choices, families turn to private schools or even homeschooling. The continuously increasing number of homeschools and waitlisted private schools since the pandemic demonstrates a growing demand for change.

What Is Culture For?

"Culture expresses goals through values and beliefs and guides activity through shared assumptions and group norms."
—The Culture Factor

Since the pandemic, the number of families attending public school in my city has been in decline. The changing demographics due to the increasing cost of living in the city is one reason to blame. Another suggested reason by some is the lower birth rate. However, when we learned that enrollment at private schools and homeschooling hit an all-time high for the same period over the same area, I couldn't help but doubt if the lower birth rate was to blame. The hard truth is that the public school system has been losing its attractiveness.

The local school culture serves the purpose of the school system: to supply a workforce for society. Yet many jobs either no longer exist or have changed drastically. The emerging jobs require different skill sets, mentalities, and knowledge. The purpose of the school system was set in motion in the '60s and still hasn't been changed. Remember what we saw from *Waiting for "Superman"*:

> *"Schools like Woodside are doing the job they were designed for fifty years ago. The system of tracking fits the demands of the time. Only **20 percent** of high school graduates are expected to go to college. They will become doctors, lawyers, and CEOs. The **next 20 percent** are meant to go straight into skilled jobs like accountants, managers, and bureaucrats. And the **bottom 60 percent** become workers like farmers and factory workers. There were jobs for everyone in the booming post-war economy, and schools like Woodside did their part to supply a useful workforce. The problem is our schools haven't changed, but the world around them has."*

As we mentioned at the start of this chapter, a helpful lens for examining culture is asking whether it serves the system's purpose and goals. The school culture that we inherited more than 60 years ago served the purpose of workforce supply in the industrial age but appears to be more and more at odds with everything else in today's world. Pedagogy is one thing, but the environment is just as important when it comes to influencing and contributing to school outcomes.

Again, when we pay attention to cultural styles, the question is *not* about which one is good or bad, but whether a cultural style serves the people it is intended to. They might work for some systems in some eras, but what do our children and their learning needs require?

With this gap in culture in mind, I couldn't help but turn to the institutions and organizations that have done it differently, to learn from their examples. Akimbo and Summit Public

Schools have demonstrated that it's possible to build a community-focused model with a different culture style than other schools or even what popular culture has defaulted to. Building culture starts with a clear purpose.

Chapter 11:
The Learning Culture

"College. Career. Life. Equipping every student to lead a fulfilled life."
—Summit Public Schools

The above statement is on Summit's website, and reading it was the first time I felt like a school cared about my children beyond college. *A fulfilled life.* It resonates not just because it names everyone's true purpose in life—fulfillment—but because it speaks to people like us who consider ourselves lifelong learners.

Instead of believing the purpose of school is simply to help children go to college and find a job, maybe the answer to "What is school for?" is that it's for *life*. And if a fulfilled life is the end, college and career opportunities are the means to that end. Learning and studying activities will be organized differently based on what is considered a means and what is an end, and what kind of environment and culture those means occur in.

Both Summit Public Schools and Seth Godin's Akimbo Workshops operate in a Learning culture which, like other culture styles, has its pros and cons. Recall the description from the Culture Factor study:

Learning *is characterized by exploration, expansiveness, and creativity. Learning environments are inventive and open-minded places that spark new ideas and encourage people to explore alternatives. Employees are united by curiosity; leaders emphasize innovation, knowledge, and adventure.*

Advantages: Improved innovation, agility, and organizational learning.

***Disadvantages:** Overemphasis on exploration may lead to a lack of focus and an inability to exploit existing disadvantages.*

The biggest difference between change-resilient culture styles like Learning, Purpose, and Enjoyment is that they serve people by learning about them and making changes that better serve their purposes and goals, instead of only prioritizing the system's stability.

While it will look different for every organization, Caring and Results are expected in every organization. With Caring and Results as the axis, Learning culture is the middle ground where interdependence and individual achievement meet and support each other.

Studying in the Learning Culture

It's natural to believe learning activities would go well in an environment running on the Learning culture. But what about studying? How do schools with project-based learning make sure that students meet grade standards on subjects like math, reading, science, history, etc.? This is a worry that some parents have, but seeing how studying is organized at Summit addresses those concerns.

Remember, there are two kinds of projects at Summit: studying projects and interest-based learning projects (Expedition). The former is required, with no choice, and graded, while the latter is required to participate, but students are given full autonomy and choice, and they are not graded. Studying projects teach subjects like English, history, etc., but instead of organizing them as individual classes, they are structured as projects with a start and end timeframe, sections to complete, and autonomy for students to prioritize their work based on their own studying pace, strengths, and understanding.

In a Learning culture, studying is crucial, but not for testing. Studying is a way to figure out problems. When the goal is for students to further their learning experiences so they are equipped to reach their dreams, students are more motivated to study. They will enroll in the process to build the ladder to reach their dreams more than they will enroll for passing standardized tests. In fact, in Washington State, Summit Public Schools don't use standardized test results for their school goals at any level. The only reason they require students to take those tests is to meet state laws and regulations.

Study-based subjects in a Learning culture are graded, but the grades aren't defined by tests. They are indicators of the information digested and absorbed, and students have opportunities to improve their grades for all their studying projects. Instead of working up to a one-time assessment, students can keep improving within the project timeframe.

Success doesn't mean the highest grades but the improvement from where students were to where they are at the end of the school year. Making progress is emphasized more than getting a good grade.

The status in this kind of culture isn't about who gets ahead or has the highest grade, but who is available to help peers in need with their studying. Each student's studying platform at Summit has the option to label themselves as "available to help others" when they have completed their studying. This allows them to offer to help those who aren't yet done so that everyone can get ahead. At the same time, mentors (teachers) follow the same group of students through all of their middle school years, offering consistent care and long-term support instead of the one-year turnover that is common practice in other schools.

Studying is an important part of project-based learning and is the foundation students can build their future upon. But in a Learning culture, studying is organized to become that foundation for all students, regardless of whether they are academically oriented.

How Learning Is Organized

The goal for learning projects is never about compliance; choice and autonomy are core components. At the same time, learning projects like Expedition are not extracurricular. They are a part of the curriculum during school hours, and every student has access to them. Students have full autonomy to decide which project they want to do, and the choices are abundant. Summit encourages students to come up with their own projects, and mentors work with students to develop them. According to Adam Grant in *Hidden Potential*, "Extensive evidence shows that the wellspring of intrinsic motivation is having the freedom of opportunity to explore our interests." By giving students a sense of agency to create their own learning experience, Summit can help everyone achieve their studying and learning results.

Unlike students at our neighborhood school, students at Summit aren't taken out of their school routines for months to prepare for standardized tests, but Summit results are still remarkable: 96 percent of graduates are accepted to a four-year college, and Summit alumni go on to complete college at two times the rate of the US national average.

Because of this goal, learning projects are not designed to measure students but to help them connect to themselves through their passions and interests. Learning projects never show up on report cards. Period. Some parents have worried that their children wouldn't learn anything without having the proof in grading. This is understandable, but it misses an important truth about the ways people interact in a community setting.

Recall the example of Gore in chapter eight: The company demonstrates that, in small groups, informal personal relationships are many, many times more effective than larger, impersonal groups. When everybody knows everybody, peer pressure is much more powerful than the rules imposed on people "because we want to live up to what is expected of us." When groups are smaller and closer and there is no grading in learning, students are more relaxed, willing to connect, and open to helping each other. Getting ahead alone is no longer the only way students are rewarded. This combination of community focus and shifted rewards encourages personal achievement as well as a community spirit where contribution and teamwork are emphasized.

At Summit, even the middle school year-end celebration is centered on learning. Instead of rewarding favoritism and popularity, there are two parts to the celebration. One part was for students to show their work, presenting a book report or an essay based on a book they read, mathematics work such as a triangle rooftop made using trigonometry, and various creations such as remote-controlled robotic cars. The award ceremony celebrates individuals who won the Kindness challenge by demonstrating pro-social skills such as understanding and managing their feelings, making friends and being a friend, and solving social challenges, as well as the collective—the pods (classroom) that have shown the best teamwork, such as winning the trivia game competition, having the "best Halloween decorations," to name a few.

This event reminded me of the year-end celebration at Hogwarts, where Gryffindor, Slytherin, Ravenclaw, and Hufflepuff's flags unfolded as each award was announced. There were no cohort flags at Summit, but the vibe, values, and love from everyone there (families were invited to attend and witness) were buzzing and blossoming in the air. It felt truly magical.

I realized this was what belonging looked and felt like. It was what I had looked for since the beginning of our school journey. This quiet alignment filled my heart and spirit, making the experience of observing as parents just as exciting and fulfilling as the satisfaction the students, mentors, and staff seemed to enjoy.

Failure in Learning Culture

When students sign up to explore something that might not work, without the pressure of impending grades, they learn how to fail. In fact, some students sign up to learn a topic like gaming only to find out that, even though the idea seemed pretty cool, they are not interested in the coding that's required in it. By "failing" to enjoy that subject, they learn that gaming isn't just about looking cool and smart. More importantly, students learn about themselves as they connect (or not) to each learning project.

When we were in the hardest part of learning podcasts in the Akimbo Workshop, one of my peers shared a video about failure. In it, Spanx CEO Sara Blakely talked about her definition of failure while growing up. She explained that her dad redefined failure for her in a way that affected her entire life: Instead of just asking her and her brother about things that went well, he encouraged them to talk about the things that they tried but didn't work. Each time, her father was delighted to hear their stories about what didn't work out. To further anchor the lesson, he was disappointed when they had nothing to share that week. She said the ultimate lesson was that "failure isn't about the outcome, but not trying."

In his workshops, Seth Godin encourages students to try something that might not work and emphasizes the importance of enrollment in learning, which includes embracing failure. He says that "when failure isn't an option, neither is success."

Unlike studying, failing in a safe environment is one of the most important goals for learning.

Volunteering in Learning Culture

Peer support and mentor support are vital to project-based learning, and I have observed that parent volunteers are much less needed or are needed for a very different purpose.

Over the years, among the parents I have observed as active school volunteers or those who have chosen to speak up, a few were simply following the tradition of volunteering. But many parents were showing up just to make sure that their children were seen, understood, and supported by the school system—either out of fear based on their lived experiences or from evidence that told them something wasn't working. They were seeking the peace of mind that every parent wants for their children.

Schools like Summit do need parents' advocacy at the state level and in outreach such as setting up a school presence at community events to answer questions and connect with potential students and families. But within a culture that already prioritizes individual children and ensures they are seen and supported, parental involvement looks very different.

In a project-based learning school, the parents' involvement is by invitation only and much less common. Few people complain about how much they are asked to do. Volunteering needs decline further as parents experience remarkable changes in their students. Schools that operate in a Learning culture help students build their individual status through personal care, group work, and self-reliance. Taking accountability for their learning and studying while also helping them accept themselves and each other creates the peace of mind that parents seek.

An Opportunity to Dream

When I asked my child to tell me one thing that he liked the most during his most recent year at Summit, he said it was Expedition (his learning projects). Why? "Because it's fun."

Yes, learning leads to results—but perhaps the best result of all is when the process of learning is joyful.

The first question students answer to themselves is what they want to be when they grow up, then they get to share their dreams with their mentor, each other, and their family members. Their learning and studying are then driven by their dreams, with every new milestone taking them one step closer to fulfilling them. And when everyone gets to be themselves, go after their dreams, *and* appreciate each other for who they truly are, what greater joy can we ask for?

There is the joy of students doing what they are interested in doing. Then there is the joy of being themselves, with the agency to claim what they like, discover who they are, and dream about their future.

Opportunities to dream not only give students a chance to see their possibilities for the future, but also unlock motivation, ownership, and emotional enrollment. They help students see studying through a totally different lens—no longer something they have to do for a teacher, parents, or someone else, but for themselves and their future. Picture kids dreaming together, walking alongside each other while imagining the future. That's a powerful image that we would all love to see, support, and advocate for.

When I asked my peers from Akimbo Workshops the same question—what did they enjoy most?—almost everyone remarked about the amount of care, generosity, and love they experienced in the community. The workshops helped people write books, screenplays, songs, albums, and blogs. They launched websites, podcasts, workshops, and online courses. Akimbo students were creating and shipping work every day, but the results that mattered were when people could find connections, support each other, and show that they cared.

When a Learning culture considers the uniqueness of each child—both their interests and their pace of learning—students feel less anxious about being true to themselves, with no need to run around trying to be like someone else, and more certain and trusting within their environment. This also releases the parents' need to fight for a teacher's attention or a certain placement, level, or treatment. Real safety doesn't come from attendance as the way it has been measured, but the joy each person experiences, their connection with self and others, and mutual trust with the peers and mentors that the community set out to learn about, accept, and nurture.

Warmth, collaboration, and values like generosity and support allow students to take risks, fall down, and get back up again and again. This provides the conditions for resilience, which doesn't come from successes, but constant exposure to challenges. It prepares students to face the unpredictable future ahead of them— and on top of all of that, it ensures learning is *fun*.

Dreaming while learning unlocks motivation and ownership toward studying, and the change is profound in many ways. Not only do students discover a sense of agency and see the purpose of studying, but with the end so clearly in mind, they begin to explore the means such as college and career choices as early as sixth grade. Instead of assuming what life beyond high school will be, Summit students get to explore their options for seven years before college. As a result, 96 percent of all Summit graduates are four-year college-ready and as students who have learned how to learn, college isn't the only path available.

Maybe, before offering studying and learning, the purpose of our schools is to simply accept that human beings come in all shapes and sizes, with beautiful and diverse intelligence and emotional well-being. Until our schools genuinely accept students as who they are born to be, it will be challenging to meet their needs as whole human beings.

Support for Success

Curriculum and structure alone aren't enough to make project-based learning a success. This kind of system cannot work without a culture and community to support it. To make studying work within project-based learning, two kinds of support are needed: mentor and peer-to-peer.

Recall that homeroom teachers at Summit are called "mentors," and each mentor is in charge of a certain number of students for their entire middle school or high school years. Adam Grant called this "looping" in his New York Times article, *What Most American*

Schools Do Wrong[15], and that ongoing support is the scaffolding for student success. This helps mentors understand each student's personality, unique learning style, and personal progress patterns, as well as their strengths and challenges. It takes time for people to warm up to each other, connect, and build trust in a partnership that contributes to long-term success. Having a new teacher every year does not allow that kind of relationship to grow.

Throughout the school year, mentors meet with students one-on-one each week to review their challenges and progress. If students need to, they can modify their progress during these meetings. This focused attention helps students learn more about themselves and their projects, and it supports their incremental assessment and progression without lowering expectations of them. In fact, Summit holds the same high expectations of every student. Mentors and coaches encourage students to meet them instead of compromising around the lowest common denominator. This is an integral part of the goal of creating individualized support.

From the perspective of maximizing students' potential, mentoring in Summit is closer to professional coaching services, such as a results-coaching approach. But instead of adults, it was designed for students. Other schools understand the importance of coaching, but few understand what it takes to be able to do the work properly. When Adam Grant talks about professionalizing teaching, this is what he means. In a society where the teaching profession is highly sought after and admired, the level of training and professionalism required and facilitated is comparable to medical doctors—and at minimum should uphold standards similar to professional services.

Peer-to-peer support is also built into Summit and Akimbo's systems. In these Learning cultures and environments, peer-to-peer support is an excellent example of helpful status instead of competitive status games.

---

15 As of this writing, you can access the article online here: https://www. nytimes.com/2023/10/22/opinion/education-us-teachers-looping.html

In Akimbo, students share their reflections by answering questions and following the prompts in each lesson, not for teachers or coaches to review, but for the other students in the same cohort. Students help each other to think, reflect, and raise new questions. People who give feedback find themselves learning more *by giving*, because of the resources they need to look up and the logic they have to work out on their end to communicate their thoughts and ideas. People receiving feedback learn to listen, ponder, and practice their capacity to embrace all kinds of answers.

It's easy to accept the answers that agree with us, but the answers we don't want to hear can be valuable too. Discerning what's helpful and what's not is an important part of learning. In this way, feedback helps us build resilience and critical thinking skills.

Understanding Customers

The biggest difference between a customer-oriented culture and a system-oriented culture is how much the organization understands its core audience. This applies to schools as well.

Students are at the front and center as the customers that schools like Summit serve. Every decision a Summit school makes is based on whether it serves students and aligns with its promise of "equipping every student to lead a fulfilled life." Having both studying projects and learning allows them to see every student as a whole human being with diverse intelligence and interests, and helps them access their hidden potential for a fulfilled life.

Summit also understands the importance of family relationships and support for a student's emotional well-being, growth, and overall school experience. Bringing families alongside students without the added influence and impact of common societal challenges such as status games and favoritism is a learning journey on its own.

Instead of inviting parents to form a PTA in the school, Summit leads parents to contribute to each student's school life effectively. During the school year, parents receive text messages that inform us of our student's studying progress (though learning projects offer so much fun, students often voluntarily talk about them without parents asking—this is true even for my introverted child). For example, one message informed me that my student completed an English project last week and that we could ask him, "What did you notice about studying this unit?" Prompts like this help us initiate conversations with our children at home. This helps us build a habit of checking in with our kids and their school experience, and it also opens the door for us to further enhance our bond with our children. When we participate in this way, it sends an important signal to our kids that we care about how they are doing at school, we value their education, and we've got their back no matter what.

When schools like Summit extend learning and care from students to families, they establish expertise through their empathy and understanding, and at a much higher level than we expect. For the most part, parents can relax and have peace of mind that our children are cared for and in trusted hands at school. Standing in customers' shoes is the most powerful way to build trust. When students' and parents' experiences tell us that we are seen, heard, and understood before we ask, the level of our trust in schools is at its highest. This is the kind of trust schools want to build with people.

Raising the Average

When my son was at our neighborhood school, he was often frustrated with boredom and thought I was in charge of finding things that were interesting for him. Not anymore. Now, when he has free time, he plans activities and organizes with his friends to make them happen. When he does need support, he asks and works out alternative plans when the answer is "no." He's always trying to do what's possible instead of what's certain.

Learning has changed, and with it, what students think about school. Learning is not about grades and studying, it's about doing what's interesting, pursuing dreams, and discovering what might not work. When schools don't provide these opportunities, waiting for permission, following instructions, and doing things only when they are certain become the norm. It's miserable not just for kids, but for the people around them.

When each student gets to shine through their strengths in sports, cooking, visual arts, performance, dance, fashion design, music production, etc.—*everyone* shines. Studying environments usually bring the spotlight to students who are academic-oriented. But a Learning culture brings the spotlight to children who otherwise wouldn't be recognized in another environment. Helping kids feel proud of themselves and connected with their interests and passions is the best practice of equity and inclusion we can facilitate. It not only develops students' self-empathy but also builds up their empathetic capacity toward peers, mentors, and staff in school.

Individual emotional security, or the capacity to feel safe, makes up a significant part of safety for the collective, which was largely missing at our neighborhood school.

While Summit has excellent results and study outcomes, what's more important is these results aren't reached at the expense of students' mental and emotional well-being, as we see in schools that only offer studying.

This kind of success, with personal results and emotional security, contributes to the well-being of the entire community. When everyone gets ahead, we raise the average for our schools, which is the step before raising the bar. In his blog article titled *Raising the Bar*[16], Seth Godin articulates the reason for this progression: "The endless cycle of improvement means that every innovation

---

16 This post and all of the others, which I highly recommend following, can be found here: https://seths.blog/2023/07/raising-the-bar/

that raises the average creates the conditions for a new sort of excellence." He adds, "A new standard setter can find a different way forward and create a different way to raise the bar, one that seems obvious after the fact."

What is school for?

This is such a simple question, perhaps one that seems obvious. But setting out to answer it uncovered profound beliefs and gave me a much larger point of view about human beings, not just students.

For some, school is for gaining skills to access jobs that are appropriate for a student's potential, as defined by the system.

But for people who believe in human potential and know how significant our capacity for change can be, school can be a place to learn how to learn—a skill that creates limitless potential throughout a person's life.

The greatest peace of mind parents have is to pick up our children after their school day and witness joy, care, and love in them. To know that we aren't the only ones who care about our children. Schools that are about students and people, not systems, make this possible. Schools that can't wait to support our children on their life journey, who imagine the unlimited possibilities our children were born to create, just like we do.

When schools, students, and parents work together, we are excited for tomorrow to arrive, because it's another day to learn together.

The future is full of hope.

Epilogue

Emotions can get in the way
Or get you on the way
—Mavis Mazhura

As I am finishing this book in Summer 2024, school closure proposals have been announced in the district where we live. More than twenty schools are going to disappear due to the continuous enrollment decline affecting not just our city but the entire nation. It's a challenging time indeed.

Amid these looming closures, conflicts in local schools have kept escalating. Parents have felt the pressure and anxiety, anticipating the impact of disruptions and changes. Even though the list of schools to be closed hasn't been announced, one thing for sure is that the impact of the school closure goes beyond that list. Parents have responded to the closure news in similar ways to the loss of the art program. Some have echoed the district and embraced the decision, some are worried sick about the impact the closures bring onto children and families, and some have been silent because they feel there is little they can do— nobody cared about them or would listen anyway.

The art program was the tip of the iceberg indeed.

For the past few decades, the public school system has demanded our children comply with the standardized testing matrix, following the measurement and reward system even though the model isn't working for most children.

Now that we have learned what's needed to support our children's learning environment in a way that supports both studying and learning, we have the power to create change. We can ground into our sense of knowing and advocate for what our schools *can* be for: a place to meet children's need to learn, including learning about themselves, in a way that nurtures them to thrive.

There will still be many questions and challenges along the way, and I don't imagine it's going to be easy at all. As a matter of fact, we will need to overcome our own obstacles and barriers on this journey, such as our inherited narratives, pervasive social and organizational cultures, conscious awareness and subconscious beliefs, etc. But as long as we keep seeking the truth, we will be on the right path.

Writing this book was intense emotional training for me. Passing unhelpful judgments and expressing emotions would have been easy, but who would that serve? My experience has taught me that when we are emotionally triggered, it's nearly impossible to believe that we have the capacity to address important issues or hold anyone accountable. It turns out, the hardest part of changing the system isn't the system, but the change needed in ourselves. The change needed in me.

To be clear, feelings are not dangerous or bad. If we choose to listen to our bodies and connect to them, feelings are important cues that lead us to be curious and ask questions. What is it that I am feeling? And what am I longing for? What is my knowing telling me? Then, when we are off the emotional rollercoaster, we have a chance to look beyond our feelings.

But until we fully see ourselves and our journey, feelings included, it will be challenging to see the world around us fully.

When we are emotionally connected, we have the capacity to:

Choose change over winning.
Choose connection over blame.
Choose courage over convenience.
And above all, to trust our knowing.
Always.

And when we learn to show up differently, the world around us changes too.

Editor's Note

When Jessica first reached out to me with the early drafts of this book, I was an outsider to the topic. She had written to an audience of volunteer moms and educators, while holding the weight of systems change on her shoulders; I had homeschooled my children for most of their education to that point, and the school they were in was a virtual arm of our public schools that allowed me to feel insulated from the system as a whole. More importantly, I was not and had no intentions of becoming a PTA-joining, casserole-making volunteer parent. While she shared frustrations about the failing system, I harbored judgment about the ways parents were expected to participate in that system. I believed in her vision, but it was for someone else to carry out. Not me. Not moms like me.

As the scope of Jessica's vision narrowed to the powerful book you now hold, my own expanded. By the time it became "a manifesto for parents," I found myself in program-shaping conversations with my kids' school. I still happily checked "no" next to questions about joining the PTA or volunteering for events. I still appreciated the complex system that the school is up against, and I still know very little about that complexity. But I couldn't unsee the factors within our school's culture that allowed my kids to thrive, and without realizing what shifted in me, I suddenly felt comfortable speaking up to protect those factors. What mattered to my kids simply outweighed my own discomfort.

Fortunately, thanks in part to the approach Jessica demonstrated throughout this book—ask questions, prioritize learning, assume we are all here to help our kids grow—speaking up didn't require me to go to battle. In fact, in the final stages of our work on this book, the school year had just started. During a high school orientation session, the teachers turned to me for input.

"Mama Sirratt? Any words of wisdom?"

This is the gift that Jessica has given us all. Not a manual for systems change—that would be too big for most of us to manage. Not a guide for effective volunteering—that would apply to too few of us to truly make a difference. Rather, Jessica has simplified what may be the most complex institution of our modern era by reminding us that we are parents first and always. Her work strips away the "moms like us" requirements back to its core: we are all just mamas and papas and babas and grandparents and caregivers who love our kids more than anything. And the schools that we send those kids to have one job: to take care of those children—the people who matter most to us—during the stage of life that matters most to them.

Whatever wisdom I had to share in that orientation session only surfaced because Mama Zou had helped me understand that my perspective as a parent matters. That no one is an outsider unless we choose to be. That in spite of our differences of opinion, our most common denominator is our care for our children. And that improving life for those children is a vision we're all responsible for carrying out.

I hope you'll join us.

Brannan Sirratt
Bee Seen Books

Acknowledgments

This book would have never come into the world if not for the individuals and communities who cared to make it happen. From ideation, feedback on writing, deciding on genre, and understanding the change the book set out to make, to completing the manuscript, editing, proofreading, illustration and design, and printing and distribution, I found accompaniment, coaching, professionalism, guidance, care, friendship, encouragement, criticism (in a helpful way), nurturing, and love. Not only has this experience supported what I wrote about—including peer support and positive peer pressure—but it deepened my concept of community and care for each other's well-being. The outcome says it all.

To my editor, Brannan Sirratt, you were the first person outside our family who believed in me and saw what could become of this book. You held space with patience, listening, care, and a nurturing spirit for me to crawl out of my shell, grow roots in the ground, and become someone who would eventually trust herself. You understood me first before you understood what my book was about to be. Since English isn't my native language, this is huge. Not only did you help me see that there is no bad writing, but more importantly you help people like me reach the potential we never knew we had in us. And there is no better way to show someone that we believe in them than the way you has shown me through your remarkable work as an editor. Thank you for making this book possible.

To Alder Van Otterloo, you saw the real reason for this book. I feel seen. Thank you.

To Peggy Holsclaw, you stepped in when nobody else was there to help. Thank you!

To The Reluctant Illustrator, I wanted to work with you as soon as I saw your art. You said yes! And I've been blown away.

Thank you for bringing these ideas to life with love.

To Christian Dufner, you brought ease and peace of mind for this project, and I can't thank you enough.

To my podcast guests for Duct Tape Rocket Ship: Weili Ge, Emily Liang, Anette Carlisle, Valerie Lucchesi, Neveen Mourad, John Buchinger, Ingrid Guo and others. Your courage and honesty helped me see the complexity of this work and inspired me to think deeper and keep seeking. Thank you.

The local Building Leadership Team at our neighborhood school (you know who you are): Thank you for doing what you do! This book wouldn't exist without your tireless work, kindness, and care for children and families.

To the parents near and far: Your love for children, courage to speak up, leadership, willingness to stay open-minded and listen to voices that are unheard, and care for each other inspire me every day. You rock!

To my friends from Akimbo Workshops: Mickey Horvath, Teresa Mitchell, Catherine Jaeger, Leslie Hetherington, Chandler Cook, Katy Dalgleish, Lucy Farmer, Simon Shanghnessy, Anat Banin, Susan Ni Chriodain, Kate Smith, Steve Heatherington, Nadine Kelly, Jey Jeyendran, Craig Constantine, and Linda McLachlan. Thank you for walking with me to figure out the practice, the change, and the big concept of genre. I couldn't have done it without you!

To my friends at Brainstorm Road: Courtney Daniels, Heather Button, Jacquie Clarke, Rick Kitagawa, Amber Field, Wendy Coadgh, Margo Aaron, Kristin Hatcher, Sue Fox , Heat Dziczek, Puja Teli, Cynthia Miller, Doug May, Erin Nicole Johnson, Xanthe Matychak, Alex Keerie, Chris Seale, Marta Charpentier, Patricia Bedard, and Perzen Patel. You are my accountability partners! Thank you for always showing up and encouraging others. We need the rainbow to walk through the rainy days.

To my friends at Purple Space: Júlio Baptista Barroco,

Louis Karch, Julie B. Hughes, Julie Rains, Terri Tomoff, Bill Tomoff, Jeff Smith, Pamela Rockwell, Kymberly Dakin, Annie Parnell, Melissa Balmer, Micheleina Charles-Hazelle, Russell John, Alfrod Wayman, Scott Perry, Olabanji Stephen, Keith King, Sharon-S, Kristine Poptanich, Michael Feeley, Kristina Horning, Tania Marien, Amanda Hsiung-Blodgett, Lori Sullivan, Pegret Harrison and Saurabh Mithal. Thank you for your relentless support and love. Let's keep changing the world!

To my friends at Acumen Academy Circles: Ingrid Guo, Aida Castro-Snyder, Sana Durvesh. You have been the support for this project from the start and witnessed every step I took on this journey. I'm grateful for you and our sisterhood.

To my friends Wendy Williams, Hillary Radbill, John Buchinger, Susan Lynn Davis, Doug Nellies, Mollie Buchinger, Willa Buichinger, and Stephanie Lee. Thank you for being understanding, compassionate, but most of all, a friend. I'm grateful for your love, tireless cheering, and support.

To Carrie Melissa Jones, you helped me see possibilities in communities. Thank you.

To my coach Stacy Oldfield, you helped me understand myself, see possibilities and grow to do the work I am meant to do. I'm grateful for you.

To my coach Lyndsey Upchurch, you helped me look into my beliefs and shift how I see people and things differently. I appreciate you.

I stand on the shoulders of giants, thought leaders, inspiring writers, and beautiful human beings: Mahatma Gandhi, Martin Luther King Jr., Sir Ken Robinson, Marshall Rosenberg, Malcolm Gladwell, Adam Grant, Brené Brown, Jacqueline Novogratz, Glennon Doyle, Jacqueline Freeman, and Seth Godin.

To Seth Godin, in particular: You have been my teacher ever since my husband introduced your blog to me in 2017. In 2021, I heard the question, "What is school for?" when I watched your talk, and it was through the various learning opportunities you created with Akimbo and then Purple Space that I have come this far. I am forever grateful.

To Mom and Dad, thank you for your endless love and selfless support. I am grateful every day for having parents like you.

To Henry, Sebastian, and Remi, you are my ground and life, my daily inspiration to love, grow, and learn.

About the Author

Jessica Zou is a mom, wife, sister, daughter, brand strategist, small business owner, and learner. A student of brand strategy, marketing, nonviolent communication (NVC), she has also been a stay-at-home mom and is a strong believer that career breaks don't break parents' careers. Her clients include a long-established public radio station, start-ups, as well as product- and service-based businesses. Jessica has an MBA and Master of Science in Computer Systems from City University in Seattle, a Bachelor of Arts with Beijing Union University, Product Management Certificate at the University of Washington, and has learned with Akimbo Workshops, Acumen Academy, NVC Rising, and Masterclass with Strategyzer.

About the Illustrator

The Reluctant Illustrator's pen and ink drawings come from a skewed glance and a wandering hand. Drawn from reflections, observations and musings about self, culture and the human condition, they seek to depict some of the curious ways we relate to and engage with the world.

www.ingramcontent.com/pod-product-compliance
Lightning Source LLC
Chambersburg PA
CBHW051312120626
46547CB00015B/2208